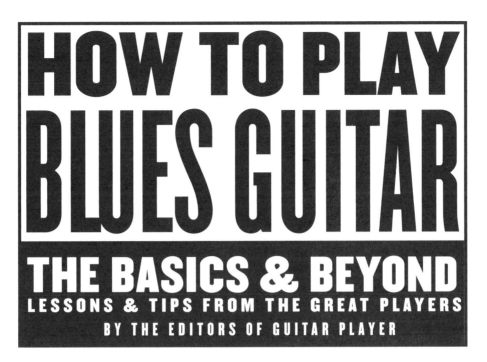

HOW TO PLAY BLUES GUITAR

THE BASICS & BEYOND

LESSONS & TIPS FROM THE GREAT PLAYERS

BY THE EDITORS OF GUITAR PLAYER

SECOND EDITION

D0851288

Backbeat
Books

An Imprint of Hal Leonard Corporation

New York

Backbeat Books (an imprint of Hal Leonard Corporation)
19 West 21st Street, New York, NY 10010

First edition published in 2002. Second edition published in 2007.

ISBN-10: 0-87930-910-5
ISBN-13: 978-0-87930-910-7

The Library of Congress has cataloged the first edition as follows:

How to play blues guitar : the basics & beyond : lessons & tips from the great
players / edited by Richard Johnston.
        p. cm.
    Adapted from the pages of Guitar player magazine.
    Discography: p.
    ISBN 0-87930-706-4
      1. Guitar–Methods (Blues)–Self instruction. 2. Guitar music
Blues)–Instruction and study. I. Johnston, Richard, 1947- II. Guitar player.

MT588 .H645 2002
787.87'1931643–dc21
                                                          2002016096

Printed in the United States of America

Contents

Introduction

"If you love the blues, you can play it," the great Chicago bluesman Buddy Guy told *Guitar Player* magazine. But, Buddy noted, there's a long road between loving the music and making it your own. For him the journey involved seeking out the masters and learning directly from them. Fortunately Guy could immerse himself in a late-'50s Chicago scene that included such immortals as Muddy Waters, Hubert Sumlin, Freddie King, and John Lee Hooker—players whose roots reached back to the first generation of blues giants.

These days books, tapes, CDs, and the Internet provide instant blues gratification, but direct links to the originators have grown increasingly rare. That's one reason it's been so gratifying to put together this collection from the pages of *Guitar Player*. For more than 35 years *Guitar Player* has connected its readers to the blues greats and their music, and this book draws from the best of those lessons. Sadly, we can no longer sit close to the mighty right hand of Albert Collins as he snaps his strings, but *GP* Senior Editor Andy Ellis did, and he brought back not only a bag full of essential Collins licks but also the inside story on the Iceman's technique, tuning, setup, and gear.

How to Play Blues Guitar is a three-part program. It begins with the basics on scales, chords, rhythm, and technique (including a new lesson by *GP* Music Editor Jesse Gress), continues with core lessons on heroes such as Collins, John Lee Hooker, and B.B. King, and ends with essential information on equipment and setup, plus a list of recordings that will enlighten and inspire you. In addition, TrueFire.com has provided an exclusive online audio companion to the lessons (see page vi).

All told, you're holding a comprehensive course for learning blues guitar. But it's just a beginning. As Sumlin told *GP*: "You got to find yourself if you're gonna play this stuff. You know what these guys did—Muddy, Wolf, Stevie Ray, and all the rest. Think about them, fine, but be yourself."

■ ■ ■

In addition to all the *Guitar Player* writers whose work made this book possible, special thanks are due Andy Ellis for helping me sort through hundreds of *GP* lessons and for suggesting the online component, and to Jesse Gress for casting his expert eye on the printed music. And big thanks to Brad Wendkos, Dave Engle, Alison Hasbach, and everyone else at TrueFire for their expertise and hard work.

—*Richard Johnston*

About the Authors

Andy Ellis is a former senior editor for *Guitar Player* magazine and former editor in chief of *Frets*. An active performer, session player, and educator, Andy founded *Guitar Player*'s Sessions section and edited Backbeat's *Guitar Player Sessions*.

Jesse Gress is the author of Backbeat's *The Guitar Cookbook, Guitar Lick Factory, GuitaRevolution, Guitar Licks of the Brit-Rock Heroes,* and *Guitar Licks of the Texas Blues-Rock Heroes*. Jesse tours and records with the Tony Levin Band and Todd Rundgren and has more than 100 transcription folios to his credit.
www.jessegress.com

Arlen Roth is founder of the Hot Licks instructional video series. He has written twelve books, including Backbeat's *Hot Guitar,* and has performed with artists such as Simon & Garfunkel and Bob Dylan. Arlen's solo CDs include *Drive It Home* and the recently reissued *Toolin' Around,* which features Danny Gatton, Albert Lee, and other guests.
www.arlenroth.com

David Hamburger is a guitarist and roots-music authority who has written several instructional books and dozens of magazine articles. David has performed and recorded with artists such as Duke Robillard and Tony Trischka, and his own albums include *Indigo Rose* and *David Hamburger Plays Blues, Ballads & a Pop Song.*
www.davidhamburger.com

Jude Gold is a *Guitar Player* editor whose performing and recording credits include work with 2 Live Crew, George Clinton, the Oakland Symphony, David Grisman, Eddie Money, Kirk Hammett, and David St. Hubbins (actor Michael McKean) of Spinal Tap.
www.judegold.com

Adam Levy is a former *Guitar Player* editor who has performed and recorded with artists such as Norah Jones, Lost Trio, and the Hot Club of San Francisco. His own albums include *Loose Rhymes: Live on Ludlow Street* and *Buttermilk Channel.*
www.adamlevy.com

Dan Erlewine specializes in new-product development for Stewart-MacDonald's Guitar Shop Supply. The author of Backbeat's *Guitar Player Repair Guide* and *How to Make Your Electric Guitar Play Great!,* he has built and repaired guitars for Albert King, Jerry Garcia, Ted Nugent, and many other players.
www.danerlewine.com

Notational Symbols

The following symbols are used in *How to Play Blues Guitar* to notate fingerings, techniques, and effects commonly used in guitar music. Certain symbols are found in either the tablature or the standard notation only, not both. For clarity, consult both systems.

4●: Left-hand fingering is designated by small Arabic numerals near note heads (1=first finger, 2=middle finger, 3=third finger, 4=little finger, t=thumb).

p●: Right-hand fingering designated by letters (p=thumb, i=first finger, m=middle finger, a=third finger, c=little finger).

②●: A circled number (1-6) indicates the string on which a note is to be played.

⊓ : Pick downstroke.

∨ : Pick upstroke.

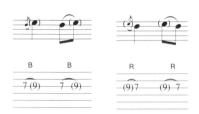

Bend: Play the first note and bend to the pitch of the equivalent fret position shown in parentheses.

Reverse Bend: Pre-bend the note to the specified pitch/fret position shown in parentheses. Play, then release to indicated pitch/fret.

Hammer-on: From lower to higher note(s). Individual notes may also be hammered.

Pull-off: From higher to lower note(s).

Slide: Play first note and slide up or down to the next pitch. If the notes are tied, pick only the first. If no tie is present, pick both.

A slide symbol before or after a single note indicates a slide to or from an undetermined pitch.

Finger vibrato.

Bar vibrato.

Bar dips, dives, and bends: Numerals and fractions indicate distance of bar bends in half-steps.

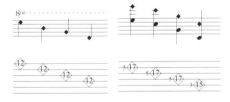

Natural harmonics.   Artificial harmonics.

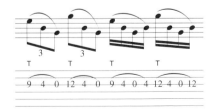

Pick-hand tapping: Notes are hammered with a pick-hand finger, usually followed by additional hammer-ons and pull-offs.

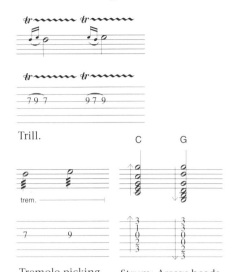

Trill.

Tremolo picking.

Strum: Arrow heads indicate direction.

How Tablature Works

The horizontal lines represent the guitar's strings, the top line standing for the high *E*. The numbers designate the frets to be played. For instance, a 2 positioned on the first line would mean play the 2nd fret on the first string (0 indicates an open string). Time values are indicated on the standard notation staff seen directly above the tablature. Special symbols and instructions appear between the standard and tablature staves.

Chord Diagrams

In all *How to Play Blues Guitar* chord diagrams, vertical lines represent the strings, and horizontal lines represent the frets. The following symbols are used:

━━━ Nut; indicates first position.

X Muted string, or string not played.

○ Open string.

⌒ Barre (partial or full).

● Placement of left-hand fingers.

III Roman numerals indicate the fret at which a chord is located.

Arabic numerals indicate left-hand fingering.

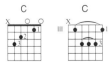

Using the Online Lessons

There's no substitute for actually hearing the riffs you're trying to learn, and with that in mind Backbeat Books and TrueFire have teamed to bring you free audio versions of the lessons in *How to Play Blues Guitar*. Performed and explained by our featured authors as well as noted guitarists such as Brad Carlton, these audio lessons are available at a special Web page created exclusively for *How to Play Blues Guitar*. TrueFire makes it easy for you to access the audio. First, look for your certificate number on the inside back cover of this book—it's your key to all the audio lessons. Next, log on to **PlayBlues.TrueFire.com** and, using your certificate number, follow the instructions to register and access the lessons. (The logo below indicates which printed lessons include online audio.) You'll receive a complete set of audio files in a folder you can then download to your own computer. In addition, you'll receive via e-mail a promotional code good for 25% off yout first purchase on TrueFire. You can use this to purchase any of the hundreds of great audio lessons at Truefire.com, including many by the teachers in *How to Play Blues Guitar*.

Tale of the Scale

Blues Box Basics

BY JESSE GRESS

Whether they know it or not, blues guitarists most commonly use three scales: the pentatonic major scale, the pentatonic minor scale, and the blues scale. When applied to a given root, or tonic note, each one—like any scale—covers the entire fingerboard and forms a movable "matrix" that can be transposed to any key. Each matrix can broken down into smaller, position-based fingering patterns, or "boxes," that typically span four to five frets. Let's investigate each one.

Pentatonic Major Scales

As its name implies, a pentatonic scale contains five different notes per octave. The pentatonic major scale consists of the root, 2, 3, 5, and 6. (These numbers relate to the seven steps of the major scale.) **Ex. 1** illustrates the step formula for the *G* pentatonic major scale.

Ex. 1

G Pentatonic Major Scale

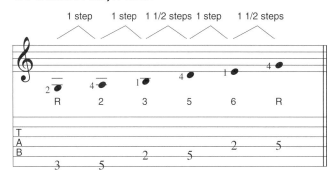

Ex. 2 diagrams all the notes of the *G* pentatonic major scale on a 15-fret fingerboard grid. Notice how the matrix starts again one octave higher beginning at the 12th fret.

The next five two-part examples divide this grid into five connected "box" patterns. Each one is followed by a short, ornamented blues lick that resides in that box. You'll find that phrases that are comfortable in one box are often awkward in others.

Ex. 3a shows the first—and most popular—*G* pentatonic major box shape. Memorizing a box's shape and root locations—the first, third, and sixth strings, in this case—will make it a breeze to transpose these shapes, that is, play them in different keys. Play the notes in ascending and descending order until the pattern becomes a reflex and you can anticipate the sound of each successive note. (Hint: Starting and ending on a root note will help you to zero in on the sound of the scale.)

Once you've wired the box's sound and shape, try incorporating motivic sequences (root–2–3, 2–3–5, 3–5–6, 5–6–root, 6–root–2, root–2–3, etc.), and intervallic sequences (root–3, 2–5, 3–6, 5–root, 6–2, root–3, etc.) into your practice routine. Add hammer-ons when ascending and pull-offs when descending, or, for a pick-hand workout, employ alternate picking to play each note two, three, four, five, or six times. Use this series of drills to memorize the five box patterns for each scale.

Ex. 3b is a typical 5–6–root–3 opening statement. Like all of the following examples, it works well at any tempo. Get all of these demo phrases under your fingers, then gradually add other scale tones to taste. Use the same rhythms with different notes, or displace the rhythms using the same notes.

Ex. 2 G Pentatonic Major

Ex. 3a   **Ex. 3b**

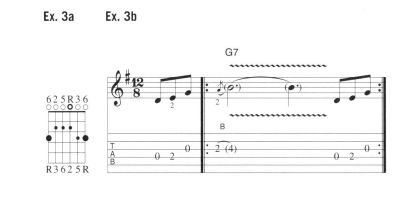

Ex. 4a shows the next *G* pentatonic major box connection as we climb the neck. Visualize the roots on the first, fourth, and sixth strings as landmarks. Glance back at

Ex. 3a and you'll find that this box shares six notes with the previous box—hence, the "connection." This holds true with any adjacent pentatonic boxes, major or minor.

A resident intro phrase follows in **Ex. 4b**. Play Examples 3b and 4b in succession, and you'll see how easy it is to navigate between the two connected boxes.

Ex. 4a   **Ex. 4b**

Ex. 5a follows suit with the third G pentatonic major box. You'll find the roots on the second and fourth strings. The derivative lick in **Ex. 5b** simply transposes Ex. 4b down one octave.

Ex. 6a, the next G pentatonic major box—and B.B. King's favorite—is home to the well-worn phrase in **Ex. 6b**. The roots appear on the second and fifth strings.

Ex. 5a   **Ex. 5b**

Ex. 6a   **Ex. 6b**

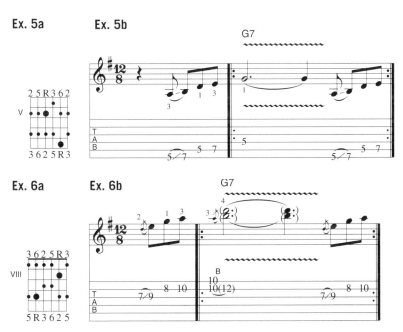

Completing the cycle, **Ex. 7a** is the fifth G pentatonic major box, and **Ex. 7b** is a variation on Ex. 4b. (Note the third- and fifth-string roots.) The next box connection begins at the 12th fret and repeats Ex. 3b one octave higher.

Ex. 7a   **Ex. 7b**

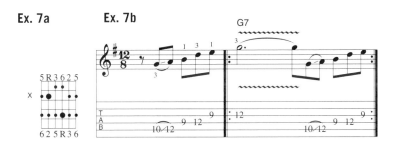

G pentatonic major licks are particularly well-suited to the I7 chord (G7) in a 12-bar G blues. While the scale does not contain a ♭7 (F♮ in the key of G), it does have a 3 (B) and a sweet 6 (E).

Pentatonic Minor Scales

Though the *G* pentatonic major scale gives good I7 chord, it doesn't "make it" for the two remaining chords in a typical *G*-blues progression: the IV7 (*C7*) and the V7 (*D7*). To deal with these, you'll need to know the *G* pentatonic minor scale (**Ex. 8**).

Here's the good news: You've already learned it! Every pentatonic major scale contains a relative pentatonic minor scale, and vice versa. Simply move the roots of each *G* pentatonic major box down one scale degree (three frets), and *voilà*—that's your relative *E* pentatonic minor scale. Or you can move the roots of any pentatonic minor box up three frets to form its relative pentatonic major scale. The box shapes remain the same—only the root locations change. This also means that you can transform any pentatonic major lick into a pentatonic minor lick by moving it up three frets. Conversely, you can transform any pentatonic minor lick into a pentatonic major lick by moving it down three frets.

Pentatonic minor licks work equally well over I7, IV7, and V7 chords. **Ex. 9** converts the entire fingerboard to *G* pentatonic minor. (Astute readers will notice that this is relative to *B♭* pentatonic major.)

Ex. 8

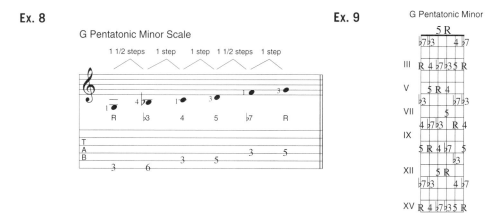

Ex. 9

Our five-box *G* pentatonic minor breakdown begins in **Ex. 10a**. While we've redesignated its roots to the first, third, and sixth strings, the shape of this box is identical to Ex. 7a's. **Ex. 10b** illustrates how cool a simple descending *G* pentatonic minor scale can sound. Try playing it in reverse or in different octaves.

Ex. 10a   **Ex. 10b**

Most blues players gravitate toward the pentatonic minor box in **Ex. 11a**. The *G* roots fall on strings one, four, and six. The comfy lick in **Ex. 11b** typifies the terrain.

Three Chords, No Waiting

Fig. 2

Most blues tunes use only three chords—a I chord, a IV chord, and a V chord. Figuring out what those chords are is easy. Just choose a key—let's try the key of A. If you can play an A major scale (A–B–C#–D–E–F#–G#–A), you'll have no problem finding the right chords for an A blues. Just play the scale slowly and count each note as you go up. The first, fourth, and fifth notes you play will be the root notes of your I, IV, and V chords. For example, in the key of A, our three chords will have A, D, and E as roots. Since standard blues songs use dominant-7 chords, our blues in A will use A7, D7, and E7. **Fig. 1** shows the basic forms.

You can also determine the I, IV, and V chords in any given key by using the cycle of fourths/fifths chart (**Fig. 2**). Here's how to do it:

- Choose your key.
- From that note, move one note counterclockwise for the IV chord and one note clockwise for the V.
- Make the three chords dominant—use either 7, 9, or 13 voicings—and you're done.

For example, let's find the three chords in, say, the key of B♭. From B♭, one counterclockwise move yields E♭ (the IV), and one clockwise move produces F (the V). The I7, IV7, and V7 chords in B♭ are B♭7, E♭7, and F7.

—*Andy Ellis*

	bar number:	1	2	3	4	5	6	7	8	9	10	11	12
Fig. 1	basic 12-bar:	I7	/	/	/	IV7	/	I7	/	V7	IV7	I7	V7
	quick change:	I7	IV7	I7	/	IV7	/	I7	/	V7	IV7	I7	V7

Ex. 11a   **Ex. 11b**

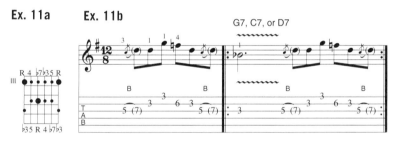

Ex. 12a   **Ex. 12b**

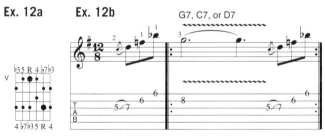

Stacked on top of Ex. 11a, you'll find the *G* pentatonic minor box in **Ex. 12a**, which runs a close second in popularity. Its roots are paired on the second and fourth strings. The 5–♭7–♭3-root motif in **Ex. 12b** fits like a glove.

Next up is **Ex. 13a**, the pentatonic minor equivalent to Ex. 6a. The lick in **Ex. 13b** descends the *G* pentatonic minor scale starting on its 5, but dips to the ♭7 before resolving to the root on the second string. (The other is on the fifth string.)

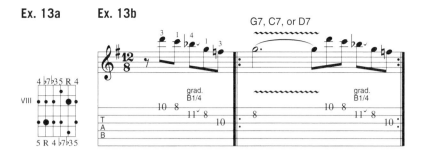

Ex. 13a **Ex. 13b**

Ex. 14a—with roots on the third and fifth strings—completes the cycle of *G* pentatonic minor boxes. Compare **Ex. 14b** with Ex. 6b and you'll discover that it's the same lick played three frets higher.

Ex. 14a **Ex. 14b**

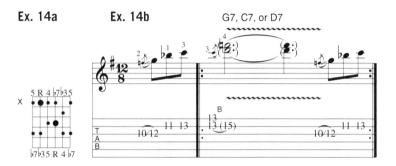

Blues Scales

The first thing you may notice about the *G* blues scale is that it contains six different notes. Technically, this disqualifies it from pentatonic status and makes it a hexatonic scale. Big deal, right? More important, it sounds way cool and you already know it! Well, almost.

A blues scale (**Ex. 15**) is nothing more than a pentatonic minor scale with an added ♭5. To form the *G* blues scale, simply insert a ♭5 (*D*♭) between the 4 (*C*) and 5 (*D*) of any *G* pentatonic minor box. **Ex. 16** converts the fingerboard to *G* blues.

Ex. 15

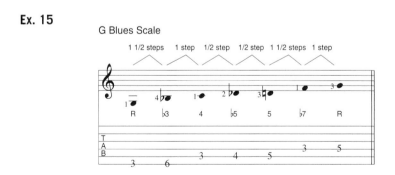

By now, the routine should be familiar. **Examples 17a**, **18a**, **19a**, **20a**, and **21a** outline the five connecting blues boxes, while **Examples 17b**, **18b**, **19b**, **20b**, and **21b** put them to use. Drill these as you drilled the pentatonic scales and savor their extra dash of chromaticism. Like its pentatonic minor sibling, the blues scale is equally apropos for covering the I7, IV7, or V7 chord.

Be sure to transpose all of the scales and licks we've covered to all keys. Stay frosty and you'll find these pentatonic major, pentatonic minor, and blues boxes lurking within many of the licks in this book. ■

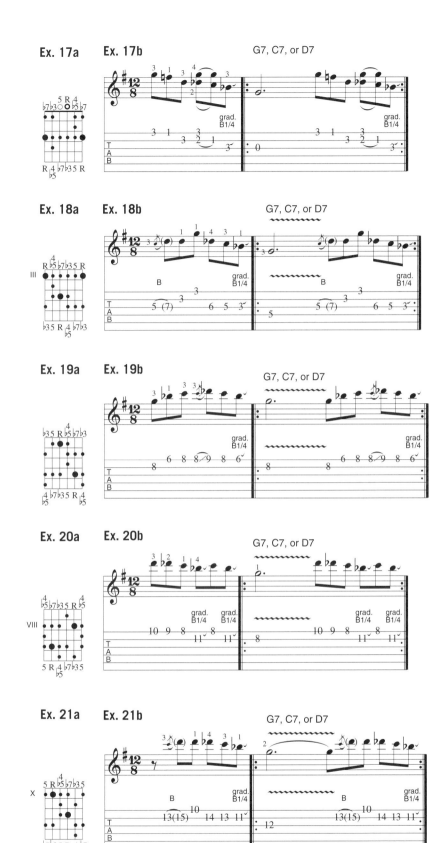

Ex. 17a Ex. 17b

Ex. 18a Ex. 18b

Ex. 19a Ex. 19b

Ex. 20a Ex. 20b

Ex. 21a Ex. 21b

Jimi Hendrix,
late '60s

From Savage to Sublime

E 25 Blues Licks You Must Know

BY ANDY ELLIS

ver hit a musical plateau—a place where nothing sounds fresh and exciting, and your fingers lead your heart instead of the other way around? To break the tyranny of predictable patterns, stale scales, and wilted wankings, you should immerse yourself in the blues masters, recreating their inspiration on your fretboard. Call it blues rejuvenation therapy. Before you start, some practical suggestions:

• Once you get the hang of a lick, transpose it up and down the neck. Free it from its key/position ghetto.

• When you find a move you like, work it out across other string sets. Try it in different octaves.

• Thoroughly integrate each new discovery into your standby licks. By linking a fresh idea to a familiar one, you'll recall the new bits more easily. And instead of playing, say, a Buddy Guy lick by rote, you'll be subtly twisting it into something new. That's good; slavish imitation doesn't always cut it on the bandstand.

- Be sure to play each lick against its indicated harmony. In blues, context is *everything*.
- Strip down your sound; cast off the sonic crutches of effects processing. Bare-knuckled, plug your axe straight into your amp and *wail*. Hallelujah!

When it comes to blues intros it doesn't get much better than "Red House." Hendrix recorded many variations (so far, we count a dozen different authorized renditions on CD): **Ex. 1** is the mother of them all. To get a feel for it, check out the U.K. release of *Are You Experienced*. (On the cover, Jimi is standing with his cape spread vampire-like around Noel Redding and Mitch Mitchell.) Musically, this lick outlines the I7 chord. Note how bar 2's tritone interval jump (*G* to *C♯*) contrasts with the descending chromatic lines that follow.

Ex. 1

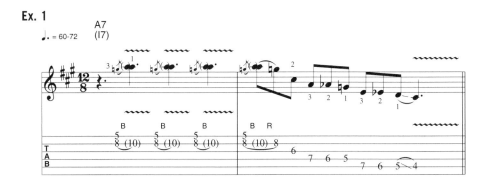

Ex. 2, a B.B. King lick from the immortal *Live at the Regal*, takes you through a tonic (I7) to subdominant (IV7) transition. Carefully observe the see-saw melodic contour; such movement keeps your audience engaged. Feel how the triplets propel your fingers into the last three notes. The lick opens with the same righteous chromatics that closed our "Red House" intro. Can you spot the other move—we're talking *intervals*, not notes—that these two licks share?

Ex. 2

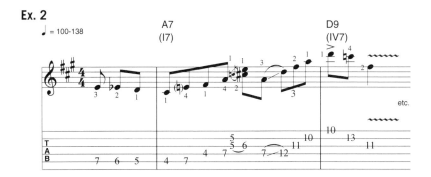

Slippery triplets, interval jumps: Hendrix liked 'em in his blues and so did Stevie Ray Vaughan (**Ex. 3**). This lick is another dynamic I7–IV7 transition. Blitzkrieg the first note by scraping the deadened *A*, *D*, and *G* strings. Don't be afraid to take liberties with the triplets' timing. Get lazy with the first group (beat two) and rush the second (beat three). Shoot for a swooping sound and put a big vibrato—*huh!*—on the last note.

In his passionate "Leave My Girl Alone" (from *Left My Blues in San Francisco*) Buddy Guy is on this double-stop lick like a dog on a bone (**Ex. 4**). Stevie Ray adopted this move as one of his staples. For an authentically greasy feel, slide into *and* out of the ♭5 with your 3rd finger.

While we're in 12/8, let's not overlook this T-Bone Walker classic (**Ex. 5**). He used it in "Call It Stormy Monday" and many other songs. (Search out *The Complete Recordings of*

Ex. 3

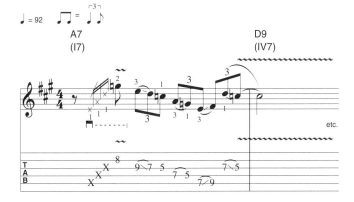

Ex. 4

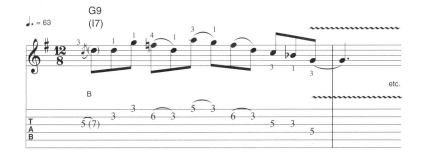

Ex. 5

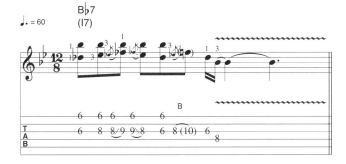

T-Bone Walker 1940–1954—a true bonanza of fat-toned, archtop blues lines.) This figure, often phrased in 4/4, became a mainstay of Otis Rush, Gatemouth Brown, Michael Bloomfield, and such modern players as Duke Robillard and Ronnie Earl. It's the 9th (*A*) that players find so compelling. **Ex. 6** is another T-Bone lick. So simple, so melodic, so graceful: What more could you ask for?

Ex. 6

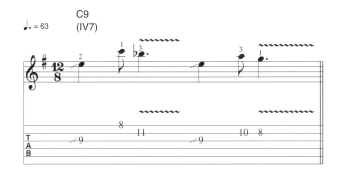

Hubert Sumlin—Howin' Wolf's legendary lead guitarist—had a tremendous impact on many players, including Michael Bloomfield and Eric Clapton. To appreciate Sumlin's unerring ear for the cool, try **Ex. 7**. This lick, drawn from "Shake for Me" (*Howlin' Wolf/Moanin' in the Moonlight*) crosses all three basic blues chords—V7, IV7, and I7—and features a surprising octave jump. Watch the half-step release in bar 2; keep it in tune, okay?

Ex. 7

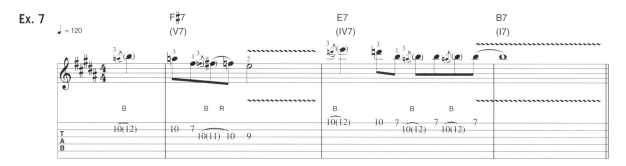

Otis Rush and Peter Green are particularly partial to minor blues. Green's "Black Magic Woman" provides a wealth of minor blues licks, including **Ex. 8** (dig the live version on *Fleetwood Mac—The Blues Collection*). In this Im7–V7 change, note how Green cleverly uses triplets to maintain momentum.

Ex. 8

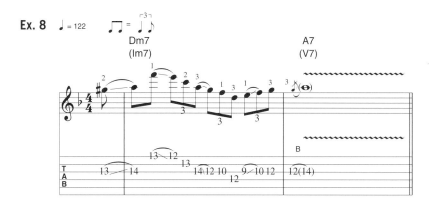

Wes Montgomery's jazz is utterly blues-infused. In **Ex. 9**, hear how he handles a IV7–Im7 change: With an A♮ against the A♭7—a ♭9 alteration—Wes proves you can go outside within a minor blues framework. (If you're unfamiliar with his playing, get *The Artistry of Wes Montgomery* compilation. "'Round Midnight," the opening cut, shows just how blue jazz can get.)

Ex. 9

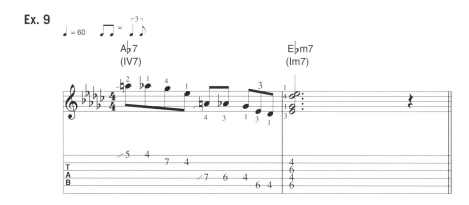

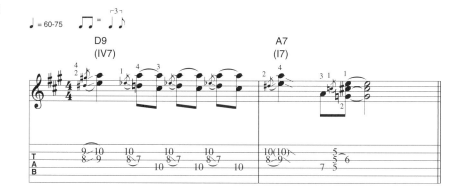

Kenny Burrell is another jazz-blues adept; his *Midnight Blue* is required listening. **Ex. 10** demonstrates how he carries the Buddy Guy/Stevie Ray double-stop ♭5 lick into a jazzier realm. Emphasize those slides to put yourself in a New York state of mind. Burrell is big on double-stops; **Ex. 11** illustrates how he uses them in a V7–IV7–I7 change. Swing easy; when you can conjure smoky clubs and red leatherette booths, you've nailed it.

Ex. 10

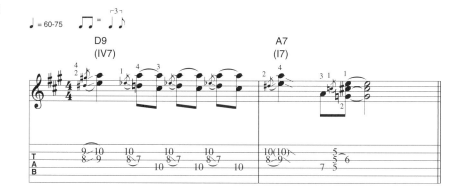

Ex. 11

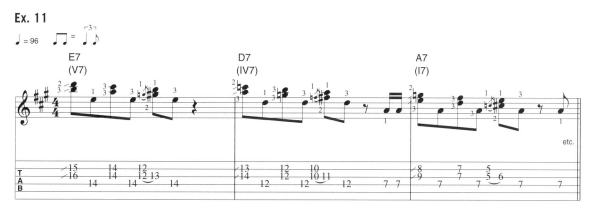

Ex. 12 contains Albert King's oft-imitated yodel. Mere mortals would end the phrase on the low *B♭*, but Albert jumps up an octave, anticipating the IV7 change with a sixteenth-note snap. This jump permeates his playing, as well as that of disciples Stevie Ray and Gary Moore. If you buy only one blues CD this year, make it Albert's *King of the Blues Guitar*. This collection contains such gems as "The Hunter" and "Crosscut Saw." Can't get enough of that whining Flying V, can you?

Albert is renowned for his manly bends; **Ex. 13** gives you an idea just how tough they really are—especially with blues-approved strings gauged .010 or higher. This IV7–I7 classic comes from "Pretty Woman." Listen to King's solo, then compare it to the lead in Cream's "Strange Brew." Did Clapton do a note-for-note cop or what?

Ex. 12

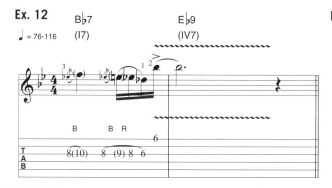

Ex. 13

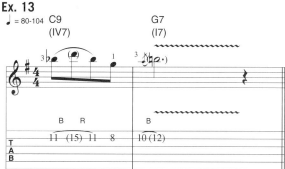

This next Albert lick (**Ex. 14**) comes our way via Gary Moore. His powerhouse version of King's "Don't You Lie to Me (I Get Evil)" on *After Hours* bristles with stuttering bends and scorched-earth tone. Keep those chromatic bends accurate.

Ex. 14

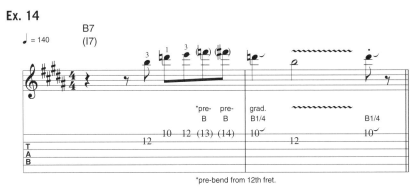

*pre-bend from 12th fret.

The classic turnaround in **Ex. 15** provides an elegant way to approach the final V7 chord in a 12-bar blues. Billy Gibbons plays this lick in "Jesus Just Left Chicago" (*The Best of ZZ Top*); it has its roots in Robert Johnson. You can approach the *D7* from either a half-step below or above (see alternate ending). Be sure to practice this turnaround in higher keys, without the open string.

Ex. 15

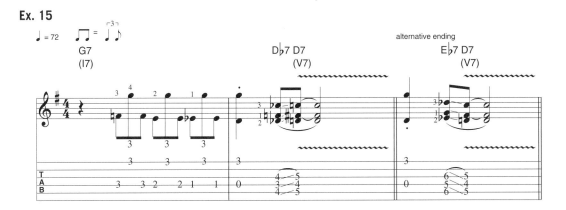

Bloomfield's exuberant playing enlivens *Fathers and Sons*, a collaboration featuring Muddy Waters, Otis Spann, and Paul Butterfield. **Ex. 16** is from these sessions: Play it high and proud, with a bright, keening tone. The 16th-note triplet in bar 2 is classic Bloomfield.

Ex. 16

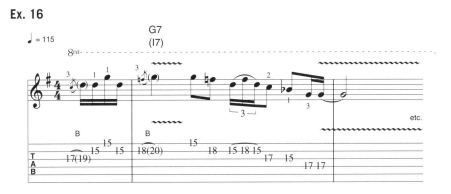

This Freddie King lick (**Ex. 17**) makes a great IV7–I7 transition, remarkable for its interval jumps and triplets. King's *Just Pickin'*—a CD compilation of his two all-instrumental LPs—is absolutely killer. One of the 24 cuts, "Sen-Sa-Shun," features the cool turnaround in **Ex. 18**.

Ex. 17

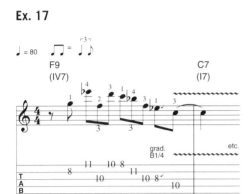

Ex. 18

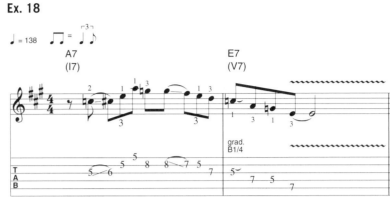

Freddie's mighty Texas mojo rocked British blues players half a world away. In the '60s, during their respective stints in John Mayall's Bluesbreakers, Clapton and Peter Green each recorded a King instrumental shuffle. **Ex. 19** is a Green lick from "The Stumble," on the Bluesbreakers' classic *A Hard Road*. Make that roll (bar 1, beat two) smooth; follow it immediately with some twitchin' vibrato on G♮. The brisk downward slide on the *A* string is very British. Go for a milky, Les-Paul-through-Marshall-combo tone.

Ex. 19

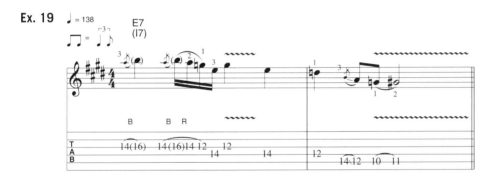

Mick Taylor replaced Green in the Bluesbreakers. Taylor's signature triple-stop blues lick (**Ex. 20**) migrated with him to the Rolling Stones. Let the first four notes bleed together. Recognize that descending roll?

Ex. 20

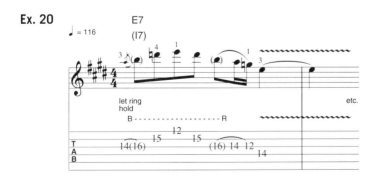

Robben Ford knows how to treat a IV7 chord. This sweet and sassy lick (**Ex. 21**) has roots in T-Bone Walker. Blues-up the tritone (downbeat, bar 2) by subtly bending *E*. **Ex. 22** features another cool double-stop against the IV7 chord. Robert Cray uses this maneuver effectively in "The Forecast (Calls for Pain)" from *Midnight Stroll*. Be sure to hear the lick against *C9*; it works almost as well an octave lower.

Ex. 21

Ex. 22

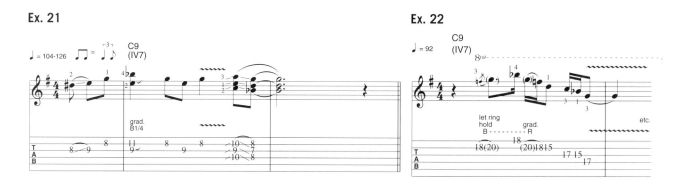

When Buddy Guy sings "I Suffer with the Blues" (*Left My Blues in San Francisco*), you just *know* he means it. He punctuates his fervent vocal with variations on this stinging, Strat lick (**Ex. 23**). Magic Sam is another fine source of inspiration. (He wrote "Talk to Your Daughter," the title track on Robben Ford's smokin' 1988 recording.) **Ex. 24**, a IV7–I7 resolution, is but one of many cool licks on Sam's *West Side Soul*.

Ex. 23

Ex. 24

Ex. 25

SRV was fond of large interval jumps. **Ex. 25** illustrates one of his favorite V7 approaches; dig the *F#7* anticipation. This lick is clearly Albert King–influenced. Play it with downstrokes and a big, howling tone. ■

Stevie Ray Vaughan, 1985

Blues Boomerangs

12 Essential Turnarounds

BY ANDY ELLIS

Are your blues a little tired? Crave some fresh sounds? Nothing rejuvenates a 12-bar groove faster than a fancy turnaround, and we've got a dozen of them in this lesson. You can use these moves onstage tonight or at your next jam session. As we learn each turnaround, we'll analyze the musical principles that propel it. Such scrutiny will help you create turnarounds of your own. So brew up a cup of something hot, grab your favorite guitar, and get rolling.

Form and Function

First, a definition: A turnaround is a short (typically two-bar) passage at the end of a blues progression that's designed to elegantly walk you to the V7, which in turn resolves to the I7 in bar 1. Think of a turnaround as a musical boomerang that spins you into the next verse, chorus, or solo. Turnarounds are versatile—you can work them into your lead or rhythm parts, and you can adapt them to folk, country, and jazz.

Contrary Motion

A turnaround derives its energy from tension and release. Tension pulls you to the V7, and release occurs when you hit the I chord. **Ex. 1** shows how contrary motion is an excellent way to build tension and release. This turnaround begins at bar 11 and continues through bar 12—the last two bars of a 12-bar blues. We're in the key of *A*, playing in shuffle-approved 12/8 time. After establishing the I7 chord with an eighth-note *chank*, we play a series of intervals that end in an *E* octave.

Ex. 1

Take a close look at the intervals in bar 1's second, third, and fourth beats. It's helpful to visualize them as forming two melodic lines. The top line ascends chromatically from *C#* to *E*, while the bottom line descends chromatically from *G* to *E*. Both lines obtain momentum from stepwise motion, and although they're pulling in opposite directions, both lines draw our ears to *E*. The final *F7–E7* chord change is a classic ♭VI7–V7 blues move. We'll be seeing a lot of this tension-producing shift in subsequent turnarounds.

Contrary motion also powers **Ex. 2**. We're in the key of *C*, starting our turnaround on beat two of bar 11. Again, we have two chromatic lines that lead to an octave. This time, however, they converge: The top line descends (*B♭, A, G#, G♮*), while the bottom one ascends (*E, F, F#, G*). Watch the "let ring" markings—let the triplets sustain within each beat.

Ex. 2

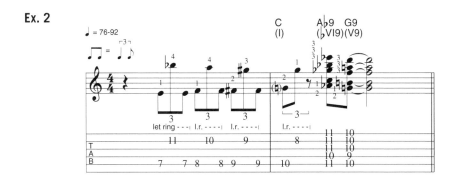

You don't have to arpeggiate the intervals. For variety, simultaneously squeeze the two notes (*E–B♭, F–A, F#–G#, G–G*) and hold them for a quarter-note. This approach is particularly handy at fast tempos. Whichever way you interpret the intervals—triplets or quarter-notes—play Ex. 2 fingerstyle or with a hybrid grip.

Contractions

Many turnarounds feature a moving line against a repeated, static note. In **Ex. 3**, the stepwise line (*C#, D, E♭, E♮*) ascends against *A*—the I chord's root. You can use this turnaround in either a 12-bar or an eight-bar blues, like "Key to the Highway." In a 12-bar progression, this turnaround starts at beat two, bar 11. In an eight-bar tune, you'd begin the climb at beat two, bar 7.

Ex. 3

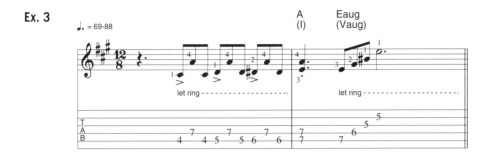

The *Eaug* (*E–G♯–B♯*) functions as an uptown V7, adding a touch of jazzy sophistication. When *Eaug* sounds too frou-frou, simply replace it with a down-home *E7*, a rocking *E7♯9* (*E–G♯–B–D–F♯♯*), or a swinging *F7–E7*. (Conversely, you can dress up an *A* blues turnaround by swapping *Eaug* for *E7*. Try ending Ex. 1 this way. Substituting an augmented V for the V7 works in all keys.)

Let's first analyze this turnaround in terms of scale degrees: The line comprises 3, 4, ♭5, and 5, and the root repeats above it. Now, try to picture the turnaround as a series of contracting intervals: a minor sixth (*C♯-A*), a fifth (*D–A*), a diminished fifth (*E♭–A*), and a fourth (*E–A*). Examining the musical elements within a turnaround lets you transpose it more readily.

Such analysis also lets you compare one turnaround to another. Take **Ex. 4**: Once again, we have a stepwise line moving against a static root note, but we've flipped the turnaround over, so that this time the line descends against the root below it.

Ex. 4

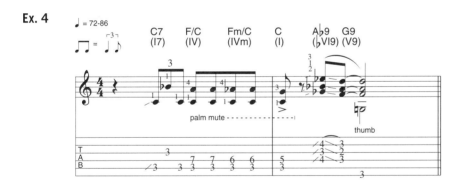

We're in the key of *C*. The line (*B♭, A, A♭, G*) translates to a ♭7, 6, ♭6, 5 move against I (*C*). The contracting intervals are a minor seventh, a sixth, a minor sixth, and a fifth. Another way to delve into a turnaround is to analyze its harmony. In this instance, we begin by implying *C7*, *F/C*, *Fm*, and *C*, a I7–IV–IVm–I progression.

This turnaround has a distinct R&B flavor and works beautifully with a Chuck Berry–style "Memphis" groove. Palm mute as indicated, and fret that low *G* with your thumb.

It's surprising what can happen to a turnaround when you shift it to a different set of strings. **Ex. 5** uses the same descending line—*B♭, A, A♭, G*—we encountered in the previous example, and we're still thumping away on a low *C*, so the implied harmony

Ex. 5

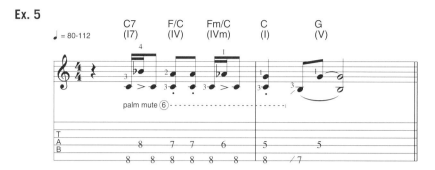

remains *C7*, *F/C*, *Fm*, *C*. This time, however, the action takes place on the sixth and fourth strings. The turnaround is easier to finger, and therefore works at faster tempos. Try this turnaround in a brisk honky-tonk tune, snapping the fourth string with your middle finger as you flatpick the muted sixth string. Pay attention to the accents and staccato notes—they really make the phrase come alive.

Expansions

Ex. 6a illustrates what happens when you fret the static root note on the first string and work a descending chromatic line against it on the fourth string. We still have that I7–IV–IVm–I progression that's been tagging along for the last two examples, but because we're in *A*, the chords are *A7*, *D*, *Dm*, and *A*. What's different is the air—this is a very open turnaround. Check it out: We start with a ninth (*G–A*) and work our way to an eleventh (*E–A*)—an octave plus a fourth—one fret at a time.

If you feel an urge to fill that space, try the spicy **Ex. 6b**. The top and bottom parts stay the same, but we add a second descending chromatic line (*E*, *E♭*, *D*, *C♯*) on the second string. Now we've got two lines pulling against the static root.

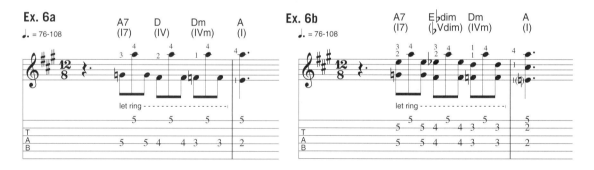

Notice how by adding the second line, we've created an *E♭dim* (*E♭–F♯–A*) on beat three. We'll be hearing lots more of this ♭Vdim passing chord, so make friends with it now.

(A note to theory junkies: Yes, I know that technically this *E♭dim* chord should be written *E♭–G♭–B♭♭*, not *E♭–F♯–A*. However, we're fleshing out the turnaround from Ex. 6a, where the line used *F♯* and *A*. For the sake of comparison, the same spelling appears in Ex. 6b.)

In **Ex. 7**, we take the previous I7-♭Vdim-IVm-I turnaround and nudge it one string set lower. Thicker strings mellow the tones, and the refingering yields a nice stretch from the 6th to 10th frets. Want a great warm-up exercise? Move this turnaround down to *E*, descending one fret at a time to the first position.

Turnaround Strategies

Although this lesson contains a bevy of "ready to wear" turnarounds, with a little ingenuity, you can generate dozens of variations. Here are some ideas:

- Shift a turnaround to a different set of strings. Typically this means having to refinger it—that's a good thing!
- Transpose the turnaround up or down an octave, but rather than slide it 12 frets higher or lower, refinger it on a new string set.
- Work out a pet turnaround in a least three keys so that you're comfortable playing it in low, middle, and upper fretboard positions.
- Move several turnarounds to the same key, and then try separating them into two parts (the events leading to the V7, and the V7 events

themselves). Experiment with swapping the front and back ends of these turnarounds.
- Change rhythms. For instance, play melodic intervals as harmonic ones, streamline triplets to simple quarter-notes, or change straight eighth-notes to eighth-note triplets.
- Change tempos. At slow tempos, give notes two or three extra attacks. At fast tempos, simplify the rhythm.
- Experiment with picking technique. Use a flatpick (many turnarounds offer gnarly string skips that are great for building chops), then a hybrid pick-and-fingers approach, and, finally, play the entire phrase fingerstyle.
- Try different effects such as flange, tremolo, distortion, and compression, and be sure to explore synchronized echoes.

Ex. 7

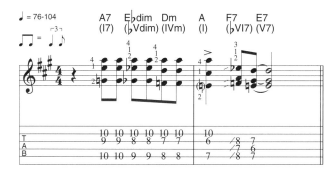

Ex. 8 proves that you can run Ex. 6b backward and get a brand new turnaround. There are differences—we're in 4/4 (as opposed to 12/8), we're in *D*, and we're ascending and contracting—but as soon as you play this phrase, you'll see the essential physical similarities. Our *D–Gm–Abdim–D7* changes translate to a I-IVm-bVdim-I7 progression. Though often overlooked, the final dominant-9th voicing is an essential funk form. Stretch-o-rama!

Ex. 8

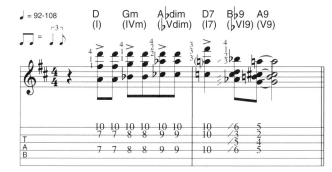

Ex. 9 may be the mother of all turnarounds. This is classic Delta blues—wide intervals and ringing open strings supported by an insistent, palm-muted low *E*. (For a real treat, play it on a 12-string.) Now contrast Ex. 9 with **Ex. 10**. Despite the obvious key and time signature differences, both turnarounds feature the same I7-♭Vdim-IVm-I progression. What makes them sound so different is their density: The harmony in Ex. 9 is spread across two octaves, whereas in Ex. 10, the chords are voiced very compactly. See how they occur on only three adjacent strings? Ex. 10 sounds great with the stinging Fender Strat-and-tweed-Champ tone Eric Clapton favored in the Layla sessions.

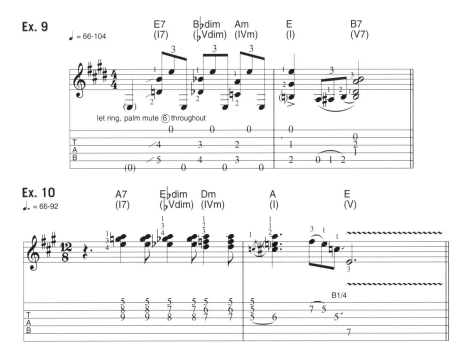

Here's the point: You can render the same turnaround a number of ways, depending on the musical setting. Acoustic blues demands that you fill rhythmic and harmonic space, as in Ex. 9. However, to cut through a noisy electric band, it's wise to simplify your rhythms and stay in a smaller fretboard area, as in Ex. 10.

Same Wine, New Bottles

Whenever you learn a turnaround, take a moment to search for ways to reharmonize the essential line. For instance, **Ex. 11a** gets its forward motion from the descending line on the second string—*F, E, E♭, D*. We're in *G*, so the line is ♭7, 6, ♭6, 5. We first saw this chromatic line in Ex. 4, but this time it descends against a tonic note played above. Here, we start with a tangy major second (*G–F*) and gradually expand to a fourth (*D–G*). Compare this to Ex. 4, which moved from a minor seventh to a fifth. Ex. 11a is tighter— perfect for when you're staying out of the way of, say, keyboards or horns.

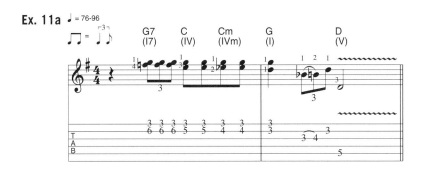

But there are times when you need to occupy more space, not less. In such situations, it's often possible to fatten a lean turnaround you already know by harmonizing its essential line with more voices. **Ex. 11b** illustrates the process. Originally, our chromatic line descended against a static root. Now *F*, *E*, *E♭*, *D* is sandwiched between two companion lines that descend alongside it (*B*, *B♭*, *A*, *G* on top, and *D*, *D♭*, *C*, *B* below).

Ex. 11b

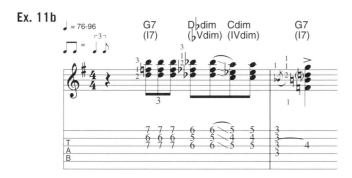

When Bigger Is Better

When it comes to turnarounds, sometimes a single, stepwise line will do the job. But there are times when a cluster of stepwise lines does it even better. Consider this: You can simply view **Ex. 12** as a chordal turnaround. From this perspective, you'd analyze *C7–Am7–A♭9–G9–C9* as a I7–VIm7–♭VI9–V9–I9 progression. Memorize this harmonic formula, and then have a new turnaround to play in all 12 keys.

Ex. 12

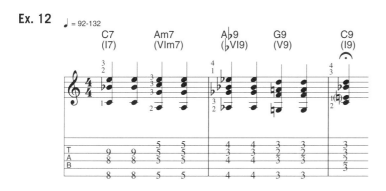

That's cool—but why stop there? Peer one level deeper, and you'll discover that this turnaround contains four stepwise lines. They don't all run the length of the progression, but at different points, each contributes important momentum. Let's take a peek:

- The top, chromatically descending line spans five chords, yet uses only three notes: *E*, *E♭*, *D*.
- The next lower line moves in whole-steps (*B♭*, *C*) and half-steps (*B♭*, *A*). It also stretches across the two-bar turnaround.
- Another line starts on bar 1, beat three, and continues for the duration of the turnaround. This line descends chromatically (*G*, *G♭*, *F*, *E*).
- A fourth line starts at bar 1, beat three, and stops at the end of bar 2. This also descends chromatically (*A*, *A♭*, *G*).

Once you learn to see lines within chord progressions and—this is important—visualize the lines on the fretboard, your playing and musicianship will take a quantum leap forward. ■

Grant Green

Michael Ochs Archives.Com

Unboxing the Blues

Adding Altered Notes to Your 12-Bar Solos

BY ANDY ELLIS

If you've heard Charlie Christian, Herb Ellis, Barney Kessell, Kenny Burrell, or Wes Montgomery play their swinging brand of blues, you may have wondered why they sound so different from the raw Texas and Chicago bluesmen we know and love. Sure, there are obvious answers: Each camp favors particular rhythms, tempos, instrumentation, and gear, and there's the issue of string bending, which jazzbos use sparingly. But something else is going on. What is it about, say, a Grant Green line that distinguishes it from one played by the mighty Albert King?

One answer is that Green peppers his phrases with altered tones. In this lesson, we'll explore these notes and learn how to integrate their pungent flavors into everyday shuffles, boogies, and barroom blues. We won't get too outside—no need to hide the children and small animals—and we won't stray from the harmonic perimeters of a standard 12-bar progression. But we will venture beyond the blues box in search of new melodic options.

FREE Audio Version Online
www.PlayBlues.TrueFire.com

These notes lie right at your fingertips—you just need to know where to look. So grab a guitar, get in tune, dial up a fat, mellow tone, and let's start playing hipster blues. The beret is optional.

Instead of memorizing complicated scales or improv formulas, we'll use an old bebop trick that's easy on the brain and fingers. But first we need to lay the groundwork by revisiting the blues progression itself.

If you play blues, you know that the standard 12-bar progression is composed entirely of dominant-7 chords based on the I, IV, and V of a given key. But sometimes dominant 7s sound a tad boring—especially after you've chugged through a few 12-bar cycles in the same key. One way to add pizzazz is to substitute an extended chord (a dominant 9, dominant 11, or dominant 13) for one of the dominant 7s. For instance, in the key of C, the IV7 is *F7*. By fingering *F9* instead, you get a more uptown blues sound without wrecking the chordal climate. This is a harmonic approach to colorizing the blues—one you probably use all the time.

Another option is to melodically add color by dropping a few dissonant notes into your solo lines. Because the blues scale (1–♭3–4–♭5–5–♭7) has some built-in dissonance, this is a familiar technique. For example, the scale's ♭3 and ♭5 rub against the I7's 3 and 5. Such musical friction is part of what makes blues so compelling.

You can take this "rub the chord" principle to another level by judiciously incorporating four special notes into lines you play over a dominant chord. Called altered tones, these notes are the ♭5, ♯5, ♭9, and ♯9.

A common trick is to play altered notes at key transition points within the blues progression. For instance, you can build tension by playing one or more of these altered tones in the measure that precedes the change to the IV. As you complete the transition, you release the tension by playing a chord tone. It's easy when you know the following "arpeggio-plus-altered-tones" technique.

For clarity, we'll stay in the key of C throughout the lesson. This means our I–IV change (going from bar 4 into bar 5) is C7–F7. In bar 4, we'll blend a *C7* arpeggio with its own altered tones and use this explosive mixture to propel us into bar 5.

Check it out: **Ex. 1a** shows a *C7* arpeggio—*C–E–G–B♭*, (or the 1–3–5–♭7 of the C major scale). **Ex. 1b** shows the four altered tones drawn from the same C scale: *G♭* (♭5), *G♯* (♯5), *D♭* (♭9), and *D♯* (♯9).

Now let's integrate these two groups of notes, as in **Ex. 1c**. First, to bring all our sounds into a one-octave package, we'll drop the ♭9 and ♯9 (*D♭* and *D♯*) down an octave and wedge them between the 1 and 3 (*C* and *E*). Next, we'll ditch *C7*'s bland 5 (*G*) in favor of the more restless ♭5 (*G♭*) and ♯5 (*G♯*) sounds. We'll shove these respective diminished and augmented colors between the 3 and ♭7 (*E* and *B♭*). This gives us a total of seven notes: *C*, *D♭*, *D♯*, *E*, *G♭*, *G♯*, and *B♭* (or 1, ♭9, ♯9, 3, ♭5, ♯5, and ♭7).

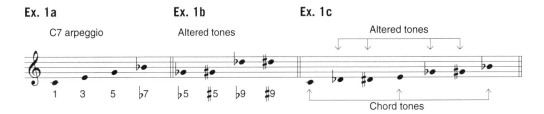

Ex. 1a — C7 arpeggio — 1 3 5 ♭7

Ex. 1b — Altered tones — ♭5 ♯5 ♭9 ♯9

Ex. 1c — Altered tones / Chord tones

To summarize: This one-octave, seven-note palette contains three chord tones from the *C7* arpeggio with four altered tones. Each pair of altered tones is surrounded by chord tones. You can think of this collection of notes as a scale if you like (astute readers will spot its enharmonic equivalence to *D♭* melodic minor), but I prefer to visualize it as a group of chord tones and altered tones that have been zipped together. Either way, we have a fistful of tangy sounds. But this is all theory until we can use it on the bandstand, right?

Ex. 2a gets us started with a juicy I–IV beatnik-blues lick. Remember, we're moving through *C7* (the I) into *F9* (the IV). Notice how good this figure feels to your fingertips. It begins with a curlicue triplet—an essential part of swing and bop phrases—and ends with a sexy pair of slides.

See how we begin with *C7*'s root and end with *F9*'s 3 (*A*)? At either end, the line is anchored in the respective harmony, yet between these points we glide through three of *C7*'s four altered tones: ♭9 (*D♭*), ♯5 (*G♯*, written enharmonically as *A♭*), and ♭5 (*G♭*). In addition to *C7*'s root, we also hit its ♭7 (*B♭*) and 3 (*E*). Cool—six out of seven possible notes.

Ex. 2a

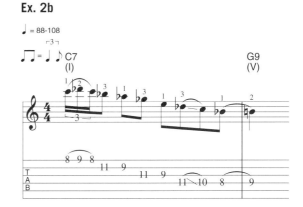

Ex. 2b

By changing only one note—our destination chord tone—we can adapt this lick to fit a *C7–G7* (I–V) change in our 12-bar blues. **Ex. 2b** spans bar 8 (*C7*) and transitions into bar 9 (*G7*). If this run sounds weird when you play it, simply strum the *C7–G7* change to attune your ears to the background harmony. Though we've just finished playing two *B♭*s over *C7*, ending on *B* makes total sense in the context of *G7*. It's the 3—you can't get more inside the harmonic pocket.

Ex. 2b shows how easy it is to transform a I–IV altered lick into one that covers a I–V transition. The next nine examples are all I–IV phrases, designed to slip into bar 4. But if you simply change the "destination" note from an *F7* chord tone to one from *G7*, you can generate nine I–V lines to play in bar 8. Hep!

In Ex. 2a we create tension by tumbling through *C7* with a descending altered run, and then release it by landing on *F9*'s 3. We repeat the process in **Ex. 3**, only this time we target the 3 an octave higher. Our altered run begins well below the *A*, quickly ascends past it, and then falls back onto it in bar 2. A quarter-bend and two slides keep the lick bluesy, while beat two's triplet provides rhythmic variety. In this example—and many

Ex. 3

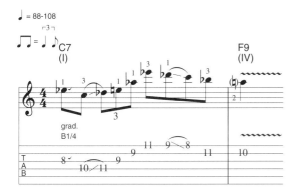

subsequent ones—the ♯9 is written enharmonically as *E♭*, and the ♯5 is written as *A♭*. Hey, we'll do whatever it takes to make a passage easier to read.

If you look carefully, you'll see a *D♭m9* arpeggio (beats two and three) tucked inside the line. Hmm, maybe that's a trick for generating altered tones—you know, arpeggiating a minor-9 chord a half-step above the root.

It's important to respect the idiom when playing blues, and sometimes a full measure of altered color is simply too much of a good thing. **Ex. 4a** shows how you can build tension in merely two beats. We're still moving from bar 4 to bar 5, but this time our altered ramp begins in the last half of the measure. You can fill the first half with a familiar pentatonic line, duck into the altered zone for beats three and four, and then hit the IV's chord tones in bar 5 before a blues purist can raise an eyebrow.

Ex. 4b illustrates an important point. When you learn a lick, be sure to explore it in other positions. In this case, we've dropped Ex. 4a down an octave, and positioned it on the third and fourth strings instead of the first and second. Techies have a saying about backing up computer files: "You don't own your data until it exists in two places." Paraphrased slightly, the adage also applies to guitar: "You don't own a lick until you can play it in two places."

See if you can refinger Ex. 4b in other ways—play the same notes, but use different fingers and strings. It takes time to poke around for alternative pathways, but that's how you master the fretboard.

Ex. 4a   **Ex. 4b**

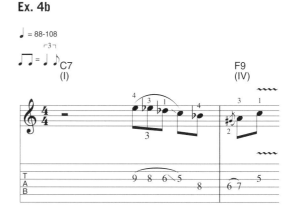

Altered sounds are so compelling that you can play them as a scale run and still sound musical, as in **Ex. 5a**. If you climb this spiky ladder smoothly, you'll have a nice, flashy way to transition from *C7* to *F7*. And played in this swinging context, the straight 16ths create exhilarating rhythmic friction. Best of all, you get to use all four fretting fingers and play all four altered notes in this "impress your friends" lick.

Ex. 5b represents the flip side of the coin—a slithery line composed of intervals moving along two strings, as opposed to a dense, four-string scale. This is a stealth altered run. Unlike the previous example, it doesn't look jazzy, but as you head into the IV, you get to slip the ♯9 and ♭9 between *C7*'s root and ♭7.

The next, closely related example demonstrates the "lick factory" concept. By simply changing a phrase's rhythm—and adding or subtracting a few notes accordingly—you can build a new lick from one you already know. **Ex. 5c** clones Ex. 5b's essential melodic arc, yet the triplets create a denser texture and buffer the ♯9 and ♭9 with more chord tones. We've borrowed the rhythmic pattern from a blues turnaround and merged it with our previous altered run. There are dozens and dozens of such phrases—offshoots of what you already know—waiting to be discovered. Make it a habit to search them out.

Ex. 5a

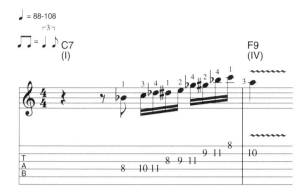

Ex. 5b

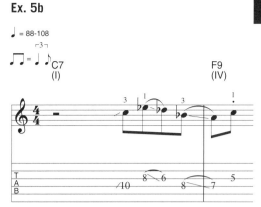

ROOTS

Ex. 5c

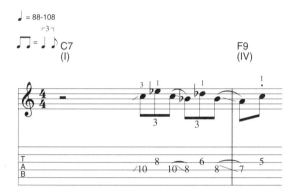

Ex. 6 explores altered sounds on the low strings. We start with a straight series of scale tones, but this stair-step approach is softened—even disguised—by beat one's slide and beat three's hammer. And here's something cool: The succession of notes suggests that *G♯* ("and" of beat three) should be followed by the next scale tone, *B♭*. But instead, we leap over it to play a *C-D♭* turn before nailing *B♭* on our way down to *A*. We're encircling the target tone—in this instance, *B♭*—with neighboring tones (*G♯* and *C*).

Ex. 6

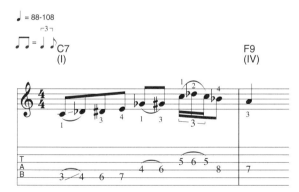

Splashes of altered color blend nicely with classic R&B comping, as evidenced by **Ex. 7a**. This soulful lick incorporates a snazzy triplet slur, edgy ♯9 and ♭9 altered tones, a greasy slide, a surprising tritone string skip (bar 2, beat one), and a groovy *B♭–F7* gospel-piano move.

Here's the lick-factory principle at work again. In **Ex. 7b**, we drop the previous example's opening move down an octave, reverse the tritone jump, and conclude with Memphis sliding sixths. Kenny Burrell meets Steve Cropper!

Ex. 7a

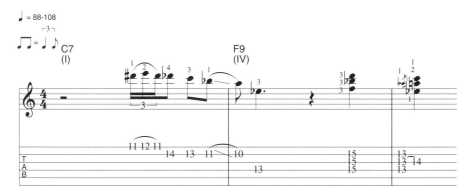

Ex. 7b

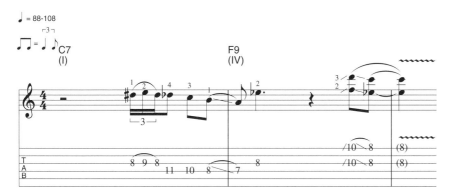

Altered Turnarounds

So far we've focused on the I–IV transition that begins in bar 4 and reaches into bar 5. Let's now look at bar 12 and figure out ways to build altered turnarounds from *G7* to *C7*—the V–I change that completes one 12-bar blues progression and launches another.

First, we need to build a new palette of notes. Easy—we'll repeat the procedure we used in Examples 1a, 1b, and 1c, except now we'll use *G7* as the tone generator.

Ex. 8a   **Ex. 8b**   **Ex. 8c**

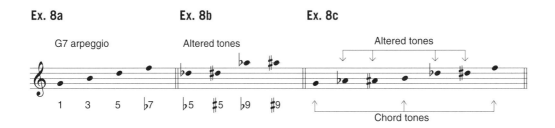

Ex. 8a shows a *G7* arpeggio—*G–B–D–F* (1–3–5–♭7 of the *G* major scale). Also drawn from the *G* major scale, our four new altered tones appear in **Ex. 8b**. They are *D♭* (♭5), *D♯* (♯5), *A♭* (♭9), and *A♯* (♯9). As we did in Ex. 1c, let's drop the 5 (*D*) and integrate the remaining chord tones with the altered tones. As Ex. 8c shows, we again get seven notes—*G, A♭, A♯, B, D♭, D♯,* and *F* (1, ♭9, ♯9, 3, ♭5, ♯5, and ♭7).

The fun begins in **Ex. 9a**, where we resurrect the melodic figure in Ex. 3. Here, we sprinkle three altered tones (*A♭, D♯,* and *B♭*—that's *A♯* written enharmonically) over *G7* to pump up the tension. Listen for the stepwise line that starts in the middle of *G7*: *B♭, A♭, G, F, E*. Composed of alternating whole- and half-steps, this line doesn't quit until we hit *C7*'s 3.

Let's try the phrase again in a new position (**Ex. 9b**). Note: We're using the same fingering as Ex. 3, but this time we're moving from the V to the I instead of from the I to the IV. Now you have two fretboard areas where you can craft variations of this flowing, melodic lick.

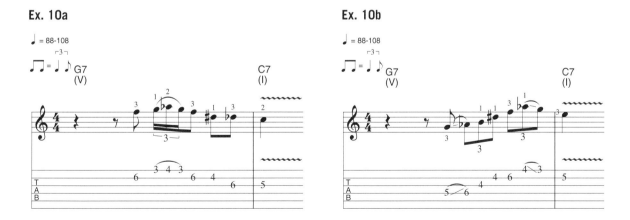

As we discovered in earlier examples, a little altered color goes a long way. **Ex. 10a** provides a quick burst of melodic tension that's released when we hit *C7*'s root. The altered tones grind *G7* for less than two beats, but that's enough to get the job done. **Ex. 10b** is another quick V–I phrase. With a triplet ascent, it opens like a coiled spring, encircles the *G* before tagging it, and makes a smooth landing on *C7*'s 3.

It's easier to sell altered sounds when they aren't heard in stark isolation, so remember to blend the old with the new. **Ex. 11** illustrates the process. Beats one and two contain an unaltered *G7* arpeggio that sounds bluesy and classic. Suddenly, in beats three and four, the altered colors appear, but as quickly as the tension mounts, it's dissipated when we resolve to *C7*'s root. Did you notice the encirclement? This is the most dramatic example yet. Before hitting our target *C*, we approached it from a half-step above (*D♭*) and then a half-step below (*B*).

Ex. 11

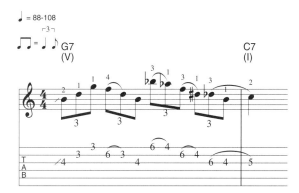

Ex. 12 has a more intense altered sound, but it still feels bluesy, thanks to its guitar-centric fingering. For more grease, play that succession of 3–1 fingerings as pull-offs.

It's fitting that we end where we began. **Ex. 13** shares Ex. 2a's construction, but we've adapted the moves to the V–I change, rather than the original I–IV move. If you play the lick against a *G7–C7* cadence, you'll hear how well the melody works in this new context.

Ex. 12

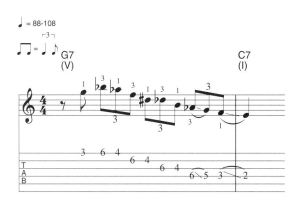

Ex. 13

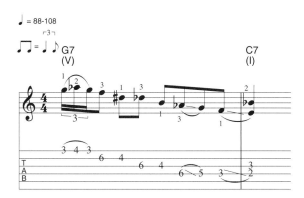

All of the phrases in this lesson snap into focus when you play them against the intended harmony. It's well worth the effort to record or loop the chords for a 12-bar blues in *C*, and then test-drive the licks over the progression. To bring out jazzy flavors in your comping, try hip V chords containing altered 5s and 9s. (For example, try *G7♯5* in the last bar of a *C* blues.)

Until you've made friends with these new sounds, stay in *C*. Once you can truly hear these lines—which means you've moved past simply playing patterns—it's time to expand to other keys. All the while, strive to spin your own variations of these blues lines. It's a gradual process that can take several years, but that's okay. The goal is to make altered tones sound organic and not like mental exercises.

Listen to a lot of hipster blues—you can't go wrong with the two-volume *The Best of Grant Green*—and celebrate the occasion whenever you successfully sneak altered tones into your pet blues phrases. Above all, to quote the late, great Howard Roberts, don't let the seams show. ■

ZZ Top

Puttin' the Breaks on the Blues

Saucy Starts and Flashy Finishes for Your 12-Bar Binges

BY JUDE GOLD

Few licks are more satisfying to play than fat, juicy blues turnarounds. These gratifying cadences please your ears and soothe your soul. But of all the turnarounds you play, are there any more important—or more high profile—than those that open or close your songs?

To start a song, you will be called on to ignite the groove with an engaging guitar intro. At the end of a guitar-driven blues tune, the band will typically break with a big crack of the snare drum—*pow!*—and you'll have two or three seconds to pour your heart out with a closing cadenza.

You may even get a break thrown at you in the middle of a tune, allowing you to make a grand entrance into a guitar solo. Why not seize these moments? These are perfect opportunities for making huge musical statements—and when you have everybody's attention, nothing talks like a tricked-out blues turnaround hot-rodded to your liking.

Granted, there are plenty of classic Delta-, Chicago-, country-, and jazz-blues openers and closers that never fail. But as tireless as these workhorses are, great players tweak them to suit their personal brands of blues. You can too. Building from phrases that have been in the blues vernacular for nearly 100 years, this lesson serves up a feast of daring turnarounds and licks you can use over blues breaks.

A "blues break" is usually more a matter of instinct than design. You just feel it coming, and, hopefully, so do your bandmates. Cueing a break is easy, and, if you're ever stuck in a 12-bar jam that no one knows how to end, it's a useful skill to possess.

First, establish eye contact with your bandmates. Then, like a singer bringing down a raised arm to signal the end of the song, use the headstock of your guitar to conduct the break's downbeat. If your rhythm section has a shred of experience playing blues, they'll intuitively drop out for your cadenza.

The magic of the 12-bar blues turnaround lies in its supernatural ability to simultaneously offer harmonic closure and rebirth. This is why most turnarounds are as useful for opening blues tunes as they are for ending them. To get rolling, check out the classic Chicago-blues turnaround in **Ex. 1a**. It's one of the world's favorite blues closers—or is it an opener? Indeed, it works equally well as either. It's just one of the many vintage turnarounds we'll use to construct spectacular new starts and stops for blues grooves. Let the fun begin.

Ex. 1a

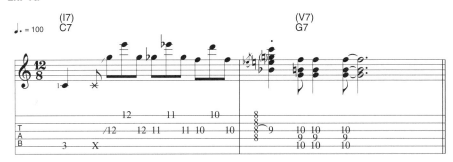

Let's use the basic grips from Ex. 1a to construct an exhilarating descent that lands with both feet firmly in the blues—and turns a few heads in the process (**Ex. 1b**). Once you get the moves under your fingers, this topsy-turvy opener all but plays itself. We're playing sixths all the way down, so try to mute the unused string between each pair of notes with the underside of the fretting-hand finger on the lower string. Then you can really lean into this riff and play it like you mean it. Anything less just ain't the blues.

As with all of this lesson's musical examples, the double bar line indicates either the beginning of the first 12-bar cycle (where the band joins you), or—if you're using the turnaround as an outro—the end of the very last 12 bars. Riffs such as Ex. 1b—blues flourishes that take place over the I7 chord—also make nice springboards over two-bar breaks beginning at bar 3 of the cycle.

Ex. 1b

The Breakdown on Breaks

- Blues breaks occur most often at the end of the very last 12-bar cycle—at either bar 9, 10, or 11. Fill them with the impassioned guitar cadenzas and/or dramatic turnarounds of your choice.

- Breaks in the middle of the song are less common, but they're a great way to launch big solos.

- Song openings call for captivating intro licks or engaging turnarounds—any lick that is strong enough to close a blues should be more than cool enough to open one.

- Before you "put on the breaks," be sure of the song's chord structure, because there are several different 12-bar blues forms. The most common is the standard blues, which is built off I7, IV7, and V7 chords (or *G7*, *C7*, and *D7* in the key of G). With commas denoting bar lines, use this sequence: I7, IV7, I7, I7, IV7, IV7, I7, I7, V7, IV7, I7, V7.

  A minor blues is built off a standard blues, but the chords are typically voiced as minor 7ths (*Gm7*, *Cm7*, and *Dm7*, again in the key of G), and the last four bars are often replaced with ♭VI7, V7, Im7, V7 (*E♭7*, *D7*, *Gm7*, *D7*).

  Finally, get a grip on jazz blues, which typically adds Vm7, IIIm7, VI7, and IIm7 voicings (*Dm7*, *Bm7*, *E7*, *Am7*). A swingin' jazz blues in G might go *G7*, *C7*, *G7*, *Dm7–G7*, *C7*, *C7*, *G7*, *Bm7–E7*, *Am7*, *D7*, *Bm7–E7*, *Am7–D7*. (Note that some bars contain two chords, each strummed for two beats).

- There is no true schematic for the blues. As blues greats from Robert Johnson to ZZ Top have proved, you don't have to stick to the 12-bar form. You've just got to have a bona fide case of the blues.

— Jude Gold

For our next powerhouse intro, try **Ex. 2**, a turbo-charged Texas turnaround played Stevie Ray Vaughan–style. If you're with a band, big snare hits on beat one of the first two bars will punctuate your entrance. The lick has two parts: the opening single-note *B7* line (repeated again a whole-step down over *A7*), and the meaty chordal tag at the end. Did you catch the counterpoint in those chords? Starting at *E9*, there's a classic Delta-blues descent on the fourth string harmonized by a rising line on the second string. To use this lick as a song-closing break, start it at bar 9 of the last cycle.

Ex. 2

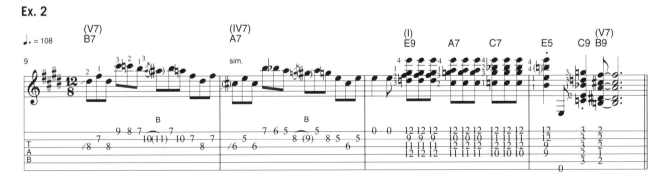

It's also important to steal inspiration from other instrumentalists' blues-break maneuvers. When it comes to big, chordal moves, pianists—with their ten fingers and 88 keys—have us beat, but we can still play wide-load grips they inspire. Ray Charles might have started off a slow blues in *A* with posh chords such as those in **Ex. 3**. This ascent makes a majestic opener, and it gets its magic from smooth voice-leading. Dig how *D♯dim7* seamlessly connects *D* to *A/E*, and then *A/E* to *Esus*.

Ex. 3

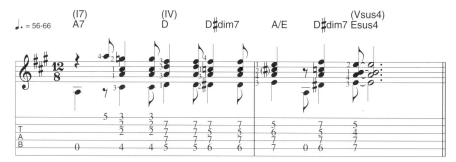

Let's rework this lick Larry Carlton–style. **Ex. 4** illustrates how the versatile guitarist might use similar diminished flavors over a slow blues. This is a showoffy turnaround, but it's tasteful and bluesy to the core. A single-note line sets things up, leading us to the heart of the lick—the triple-*D#dim7* slide on beat four of the opening measure.

Reminder: Diminished 7th chords don't require changes in fingerings when you revoice them higher on the neck—just slide them upward and stop every three frets! In fact, our fingering hardly changes when we hit *A7*. We simply move that last *D#dim7* up one fret and leave our first finger behind on the 7th fret. (Again, smooth voice-leading results in pure ear candy.)

Ex. 4 also makes a captivating closer. A break at bar 11 gives you all the breathing room you'll need, and a Carlton-flavored half-dirty tone will help bring this lick to life. Using dynamics, see if you can start at a whisper and gradually swell to full crescendo by the time you hit the *A7* accent. The band will likely come back and nail the last two chords with you. (Because we are now ending our *A* blues, try closing with *Bb9* and *A9* instead of *D#dim7* and *E9*. This common ♭II7–I7 slide gives complete closure to a blues song.)

Ex. 4

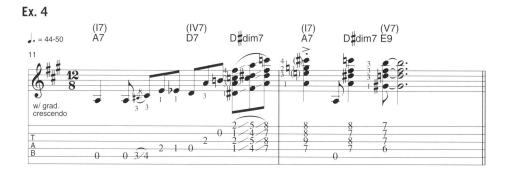

A minor blues' dark, moody changes call for a different brand of guitar break. For instance, try the four-note chords in **Ex. 5** for pure harmonic heartbreak. This is a moving way to close a slow minor blues in *A*. These poignant voicings are more than enough to carry your slow-mo cadenza, because the stirring dissonance of *Am7♭5* and the curious major third in *Aaug* will have a mesmerizing effect on your audience. A gradual ritard (slow-down) from you—as well as a cymbal swell and low-*A* bass note on the last chord—will add finality.

Ex. 5

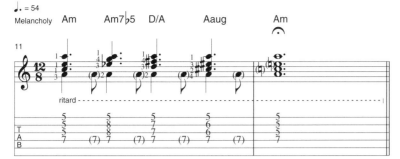

For slightly faster minor-blues grooves, try a dazzler in the style of Mr. Guitar, Chet Atkins (**Ex. 6**). This break is the first we've seen that starts at bar 10. It startles with a sudden diminished descent, but then smooths things out with a chordal epilogue similar to Ex. 5's. This time, however, our chord voicings have an open-string, high-*E* pedal, whereas Ex. 5 featured an enchanting dual-*A* pedal fretted on the outside strings.

Ex. 6

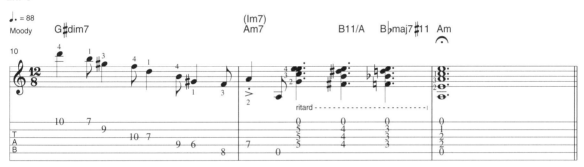

If you like hot-dogging on a Telecaster with a little slapback echo, you'll love **Ex. 7**, which injects country flavors into a blues cadenza. Based on sixths, this lick uses the open *D* string as a springboard throughout its opening measure. Try putting aside your pick in favor of a nice claw-grip attack, plucking the low notes with your thumb and the upper notes with your index or middle finger.

What is most striking is the riff's four-against-three vibe. Notice how the 16th-notes are written as quadruplets. That's because—like the rest of our examples—we're in a 12/8 blues. These four-note groupings would nestle perfectly against a two-step Nashville groove in 4/4, but against this shuffle beat they create splendid rhythmic friction. (One thing that helps you shift gears is that the band has, of course, dropped out for your break.) Dig into the big, crunchy, muted scrapes at the end, and then have the band come back in to pound that final *G7♯9* with you.

Ex. 7

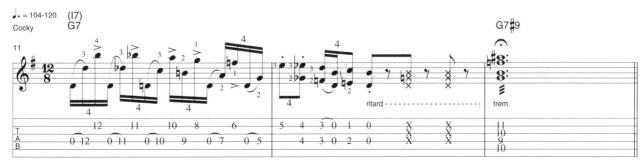

A more rootsy—but still twangified—outro is **Ex. 8**. This break begins at bar 9 of an *E* blues and opens with some basic pentatonic moves. But it's the dirty diads that give this lick teeth—the counterpoint within the double-stops absolutely nails the V7-IV7 shift. Try this as an intro, with big snare hits, as in Ex. 2.

Ex. 8

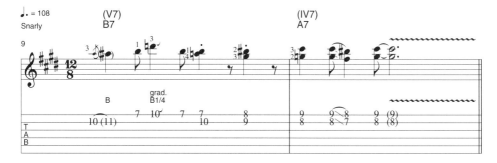

What Ex. 8 needs is a tasty tag for the final two measures, such as **Ex. 9**—a modified Delta-blues turnaround approved by ZZ Top's Billy Gibbons. You'll recognize the notes, but Gibbons and other blues gurus prefer to give the two voices rhythmic independence. The descending low voice has the typical 12/8 shuffle feel, while the upper high-*E* pedal is syncopated over the top. Pluck it fingerstyle or with your pick on the low notes and your middle or ring finger on the uppers. The voices hit simultaneously only on beat three of bar 11 and beat one of bar 12.

Ex. 9

Once you have it down, try **Ex. 10**. Rhythmically, the mechanics are identical to those of Ex. 9, but we've relocated to the key of *G* and made one exciting addition to the upper voice: a contrapuntal rising line on the *B* string, like the one we saw in the closing chords of Ex. 2.

Ex. 10

Swing-, bebop-, and some jump-blues progressions contain a shifting palette of chord tones that deliver harmonically exciting closing breaks. A fun way to handle these endings is by bringing out the unique flavors of each chord with a melodic improvisation or precrafted lick.

In an *F* bebop blues, the last four chords might be *F7, D7, Gm7,* and *C7#5,* as in **Ex. 11.** First, play through these changes and soak your ears in their sound. Then try the lick. You'll be the only instrument playing, but your listeners will still hear the chord progression because you're implying it with specific notes. For instance, the *F#* and *A* at the end of the first phrase bring out *D7,* and the *G#* at the end of bar 12 suggests the tasty #5 in *C7#5.* Close things out with the intriguing, unresolved sound of *F6/9#11.*

Ex. 11

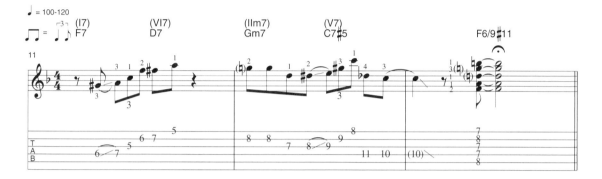

Finally, make sure you have a chord-melody cadenza in your bop-blues arsenal. **Ex. 12** is a great way to open—or close—a swingin' *C* blues. The grips are inspired by the legendary Joe Pass, and the descending melody echoes the late sax man/composer Oliver Nelson and his jazz-blues classic "Stolen Moments."

Don't be intimidated by all the ink in this example. Once you get the concept down, this lick is easy to learn. It's simply a series of descending minor-7th chords tied to a high *C* pedal tone—a balloon tone, if you will. As a bar 11 outro, this lick makes a great surprise break for two reasons: It blindsides you with chords that aren't typical of a 12-bar blues, and it prolongs the final cadence by two whole measures, making the V7 even more gratifying.

Ex. 12

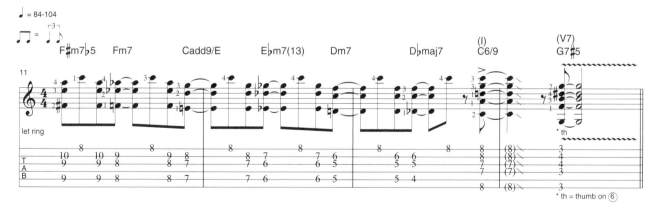

Once you have these intros and outros mastered, try some mixing and matching to develop turnarounds you can call your own. For example, try grafting Ex. 2's stinging, single-note opening to Ex. 9's customized Delta descent. Or, because most of these moves are extremely portable, try transplanting Ex. 5's melancholy chords down to the key of *E* minor, where open strings will join the four-part choir. Or throw colors from one genre at another. Who says you can't use Ex. 12's jazzy grips to shut down a rock blues?

Above all, get these moves not just into your fingertips, but up through your arms and into your chest. Find the ones that power your heart like fire in a furnace, and, when all eyes and ears are upon you, your breaks will be backed with undeniable conviction.   ■

Jimmy Reed, late '60s

Got Rhythm?

Breaking Out of the Shuffle Rut

BY DAVID
HAMBURGER

As a blues rhythm guitarist your role is to sustain the flow of the tune, contribute dynamically, and support the vocals and solos. Too often, though, players fall into the classic two-string "dunt-da, dunt-da" shuffle pattern. But with a few new voicings, double-stop licks, and bass line riffs, you can break free of the same old riffs.

The key is to use new ideas sparingly. As in any style, good blues accompaniment should gradually unfold just like the rest of the song, without becoming too busy or distracting. Nothing says you can't keep things interesting—just not so interesting that people are paying more attention to what you're doing than to the lead vocal or the solo. Think about it. You wouldn't want the drummer doing his Ginger Baker imitation while *you* were trying to solo, but you wouldn't want him hitting nothing but downbeats on a closed hi-hat the whole way through a song either. It's a matter of balance.

Your mission is make other people shine while staying creatively involved yourself. It's an art in itself, as complex as soloing, and many of the same aesthetic rules apply: Listen to the rest of the band, learn as many approaches as you can, and don't try to play everything you know in the first chorus.

Patterns and Voices

Ex. 1 gives you some easy-to-grab 7th- and 9th-chord voicings on the top four strings. With no boomy bass notes or "Smoke on the Water" power-chord 5ths on the bottom, these voicings keep things crisp and funky.

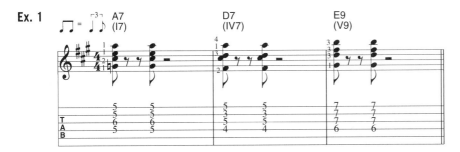

Now isolate the *tritone* (♭5) intervals within each chord by playing just the fourth and third string of each voicing on one pass through (**Ex. 2**).

In **Ex. 3** you are both the call and the response. Slide into the chunky tritones with a downstroke, then make a snappy upstroke (*gank!*) on the top two strings.

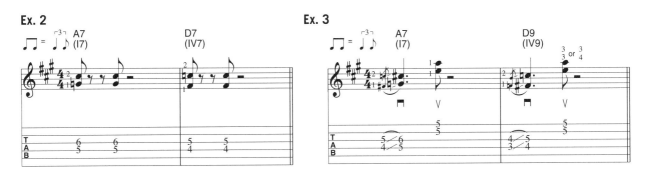

Ex. 4 begins the trip down a slippery slope that, for the careless, can land you in the bottomless pit of *busyness*. Tread carefully, though, and you can have a good time, entertaining yourself and the rhythm section without incurring the glare of doom from the singer or soloist. These double-stops are a key blues rhythm resource, beginning with seminal Chicago recordings like Jimmy Reed's "Bright Lights, Big City."

Examples **5**–**7** show three different patterns using these double-stops. You can use these patterns at the 10th and 12th frets for the IV (*D*) and the V (*E*) chords, too. **Ex. 8** shows how you can tweak Ex. 6 to convey the IV and V chords, first at the same fret as the I chord, then two frets up.

Ex. 5

Ex. 6

Ex. 7

Ex. 8

Down & Up

Buddy Guy's partnership with Junior Wells in the 1960s was marked by Guy's use of bass riffs. **Examples 9–11** show three different lines like this; get ahold of Junior Wells's *It's My Life Baby* (Vanguard), recently reissued on CD, and check out "Country Girl," "Messin' with the Kid," and the title cut to hear Buddy's rhythm approach in action.

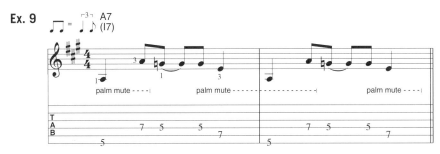

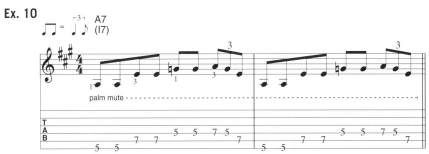

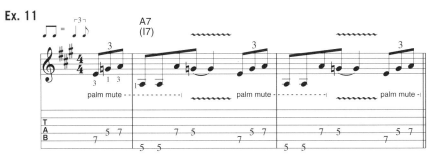

You can take fragments of these bass riffs and integrate them with double-stop licks as well. **Ex. 12** shows one possibility; hunt around for others.

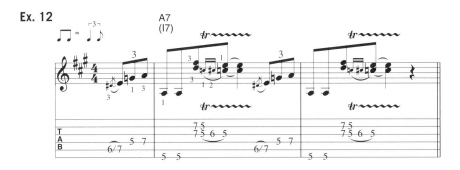

The Texas school of blues has its own broad vocabulary; **Ex. 13** offers chords drawn from T-Bone Walker and Freddie King. Try using the first voicing for the I chord in combination with the 9th-chord voicing of Ex. 1 for the IV and V chords. **Ex. 14** combines the spacious hits of Ex. 1 with a chromatic half-stepping approach.

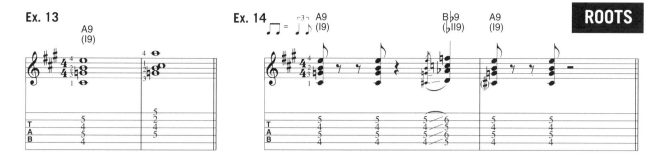

You can slide the top three notes of this 9th chord up two frets to a 6th voicing and then bring it back down. In **Ex. 15**, this move is incorporated into a swinging Texas shuffle groove. Use upstrokes for those offbeat chord hits.

More call and response: **Ex. 16** combines a simple single-note major pentatonic riff with "the Freddie King chord," the finger-stretching 9th voicing King immortalized in his instrumental hit "Hideaway."

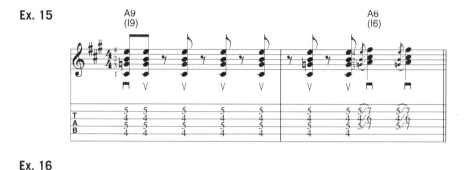

Workin' It

Now let's put some of these moves to work. Each of the next three examples is a twelve-bar I–IV–V blues. Here are three different ways to slice it, each one more interesting and dynamic than the usual two-string shuffle, but simple enough to keep the spotlight on whoever's upfront. **Ex. 17** (next page) is smooth and spacious, keeping everything within that two-fret zone by dropping that C# to C♮ in the double-stops when you get to the IV chord.

Ex. 18 starts out like a major-key version of a Magic Sam minor vamp, combining chromatic bass notes (as Buddy Guy might) with more double-stop action on top. This time, we're going up the neck to get the IV and V chords and taking the double-stops up to the 5–♭7 pair in the second half of each phrase.

Finally, **Ex. 19**, in more of a Texas vein, uses that "Freddie King chord" in a call-and-response with a major pentatonic riff, but breaks the pattern to incorporate a cool, swingin', offbeat move on the IV and V chords.

The more you learn about rhythm guitar, the more fun and interesting it will be to hang out with the rhythm section and provide the groove. Besides, it's your chance to give something back to society after taking all those thirty-chorus solos on "Red House." ■

Ex. 17

Ex. 18

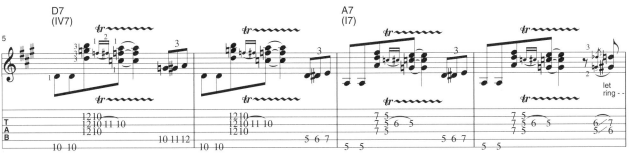

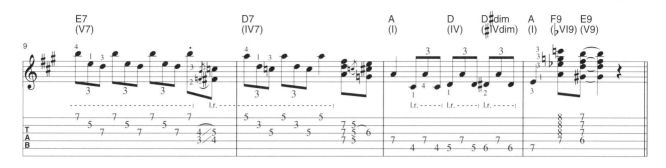

Ex. 19

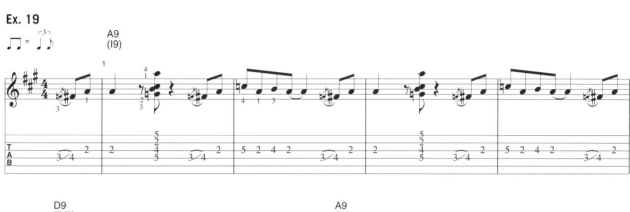

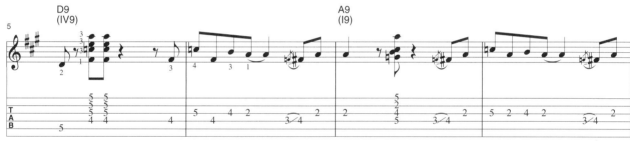

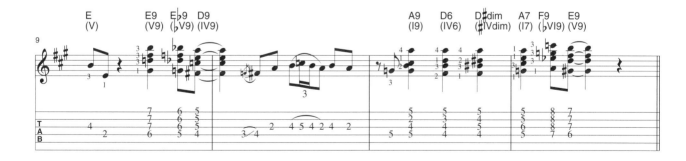

Jimmy Smith, organ
Kenny Burrell, guitar

Organisms!

Learn the Glories of Hammond-Style Comping on Guitar

BY ANDY ELLIS

Ever played through a rotary speaker simulator—or even a mechanical device such as a Fender Vibratone, Motion Sound, or Leslie cabinet—and wondered why your riffs and grooves didn't sound more like an organ? There's nothing wrong with warbling guitar tones, but if you want to emulate the mighty B-3, you have to think like someone who plays one. Truth be told, the notes you choose have a lot more to do with nailing the organ sound than with any piece of gear.

In this lesson we'll identify techniques to help you achieve a righteous Hammond vibe. Used in conjunction with a rotary speaker (or simulator)—or even good ol' tremolo—these ideas will let you step outside the world of strummed strings and enter the world of clicky keys. Even without any effects, you'll sound more like an organist using these moves than if you were to play stock guitar phrases through a beautiful vintage Leslie.

For inspiration we'll turn to late-'50s and '60s soul-jazz and borrow from the greats:

Jimmy Smith, Brother Jack McDuff, Big John Patton, Richard Groove Holmes, and Jimmy McGriff. We'll emphasize comping and focus on versatile voicings and fills you can use in blues, R&B, and funk. Good news: These moves and grooves aren't supremely difficult. In many ways, the challenge is more mental than physical. Duping organ is as much about what you leave out as it is what you include in your lines.

Guitarists routinely play huge voicings. Consider the *E*-grip barre chord: It occupies only three frets but spans two octaves. Because organists typically comp with one hand while playing a fill or line with the other, they favor chords with much smaller ranges. Although some keyboard players can comfortably reach a tenth (an interval of an octave plus a third) with one hand, we'll restrict our voicings to a less super-human range of one octave.

In most cases this forces us to comp on three adjacent strings. Check it out: **Ex. 1** shows a I–IV–I progression that's built from tight, organ-approved grips on the fifth, fourth, and third strings. For convenience, we're in the key of *A*—not a beloved key of jazz organists, who typically gravitate to *C*, *F*, and *G*, as well as such "horn" keys as *Bb*, *Eb*, and *Ab*.

Ex. 1

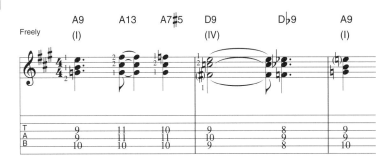

Notice how these chords are all rootless. Organists can easily finger four notes within a one-octave spread, but when we play jazzy extended and altered chords on only three strings, as in this example, we have to sacrifice the root in order to include the important color tones. In band settings the bass establishes the root, so you don't miss it. When you're practicing on your own, however, stripped-down jazzy voicings can sometimes sound ambiguous—even strange. If you're having trouble hearing a voicing in its musical context, preview its root before fretting the chord.

Let's zoom in on Ex. 1's chord tones to get a feel for the "skimming the top" approach to harmony. From low to high, *A9* contains *G–B–E*, or *b7–9–5*. Shifting to the syncopated *A13*, we play *G–C#–F#*, or *b7–3–13*. Bar 1's final chord, *A7#5*, contains *G–C#–E#* (notated enharmonically as *F♮*), or *b7–3–#5*. In bar 2, *D9* offers *F#–C♮–E*, or *3–b7–9*. We drop the same grip down a fret to generate *Db9*.

This analysis reveals something important: These voicings all include the *b7*—which is necessary to establish the dominant-chord flavor—as well as an essential color tone, in this case, either the 9, 13, or #5. For the third tone, we simply round out the sound with a 3 or 5, depending on what's immediately available within our three-string universe.

Notice how fretting each voicing requires only two fingers—sweet! Also dig how the chords change using half- or whole-steps. Though guitarists often swoop up and down the neck to change chords, keyboardists rely on tightly controlled stepwise moves to work through a progression. To emulate organ, we have to adopt this voice-leading mindset.

Ex. 2 shows a V–IV–I cadence in the key of *A*. We're still using rootless chords on the fifth, fourth, and third strings. Our prickly *E7#9* (*G#–D–F* double-sharp) is composed of the 3, *b7*, and *#9*. The following *E9* voicing is an old friend (we played it in Ex. 1 as *D9* and *Db9*), but bar 2's *D11* is new: *G–C–F#* translate to *11–b7–3*. We analyzed the last two chords—*D9* and *A9*—in the previous progression.

Organic Secrets and Timbral Tips

The single most important faux-organ principle is to keep chord voicings within a one-octave range. Here are several other tips to bear in mind as you work through these examples.

- Unlike, say, cocktail piano with its lush, rippling arpeggios, soul-jazz organ features funky chordal jabs. To recreate this effect, pluck the notes in each voicing simultaneously, using a hybrid (flatpick plus middle and ring fingers) or straight fingerstyle picking-hand technique. The chords need to spring out as chunky blocks of sound.
- Once you've attacked the strings, leave them alone—don't add finger vibrato and stay clear of your whammy bar. Most of us add vibrato unconsciously, so this means fighting an ingrained habit.
- An organ's keys aren't velocity sensitive, which means that, unlike a piano, they don't register dynamics. On a B-3, for example, notes are either on or off—they won't swell or fade without the help of a volume pedal. Because guitar strings are extremely dynamic, it helps to tame these level fluctuations with some light compression. Too much compression will take you into the realm of bowed strings—you don't want that. Instead, just try to knock the spike off your attack and fatten up the immediate decay.
- When playing organ-style riffs, avoid open strings. While the timbral differences between fretted and non-fretted notes can be gorgeous in other settings, in this case you want your notes to sound as uniform as possible.
- Approach slides carefully. Sometimes organists gliss from point to point, but when they do, you can hear each key they cross as a distinct pitch—it's the nature of the beast and its switches. You know those little whups and zings that make blues guitar sound so vocal? When you're playing "organically," they're taboo. If you must slide, make it brief, restrict yourself to one string, and make sure you can hear all the notes as you glide along the fretboard.

— Andy Ellis

Ex. 2

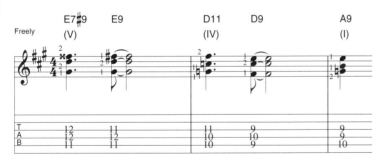

With these two examples, you now have the means to comp an organ-approved 12-bar blues in the key of *A*. And guess what? If you can comp in one key, you can comp in all 12. It's well worth the effort to memorize all six of these two-fingered voicings and learn where they lie in all your favorite keys.

Inspired by Big John Patton's "Let 'Em Roll," **Ex. 3** illustrates the kind of harmonic stabs that form the backbone of many organ grooves. In bar 1, notice how the same grip yields two different chords—*G9* and *G6*. The first voicing is rootless: *F–A–D*, or ♭7–9–5. The second is *G–B–E*, or 1–3–6. Composed of perfect fourths, bar 2's *G11* has an open, restless sound.

Find the top note in each of these four chords, and then play the tones as a line (*D, E, F, E*). This is the same figure (5, 6, ♭7, 6) Chuck Berry uses to underpin his classic rock 'n' roll guitar grooves, but in this case, it rides on top of the harmony. The parenthetical low notes indicate a bass run played on organ pedals. To emulate their dark tone, palm mute the sixth string.

Ex. 3

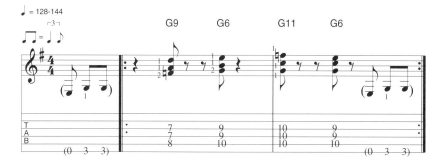

Tasty chord-based fills are crucial to soul-jazz organ comping, and **Ex. 4** illustrates an essential move. The first three chords in this phrase form a gospel-tinged I7–IV–I7 (C7–F–C7) shift. Keep those hammers on ♭3–♮3 (E♭–E♮) and 6–♭7 (A–B♭) crisp—organ keys are on/off switches—and play with a swing feel.

This soulful passage starts on the root, so it's easy to work it out in other keys. For example, begin with F♯ on the fourth string, play the riff a few times, and then repeat the process one fret higher in G. Keep climbing chromatically until you reach F at the 15th fret. To learn how to weave variations of this passage, listen to Jimmy Smith's tune "The Sermon."

Ex. 4

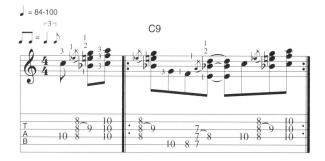

The bluesy moves in **Ex. 5** occur in a region that feels unfamiliar to many guitarists. We're in the key of G. So where's the first place you'd land to pick a G blues—the third position, minor pentatonic box? Yeah, me too. But this certified Hammond lick lies in the fifth position. Here, two frets higher, everything looks different, but it's still G blues territory.

One advantage of this "*über* blues box" is that you can use your 1st and 2nd fingers for the ♭5 hammer and pull. This results in a strong, defined double-stop sound that's in keeping with our on/off switch concept. In bar 1, beats two and three, we suggest the IV by twice fretting C–E with a 1st-finger partial barre. Notice how playing in the fifth position makes it easier to jump to the seventh-position G9. Get comfortable with this region, as it plays a pivotal role in other faux-organ licks.

Ex. 5

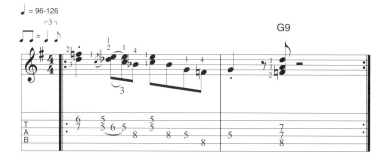

Ex. 6 is inspired by Brother Jack McDuff's "Screamin'"—though all the greats play this lick, and it likely originated with Jimmy Smith. We first saw the I7–IV gambit in Ex. 4. But here, instead of returning to the I7, we press on to bar 1's tremoloed minor third (*D–F*). Organists perform this as a trill, but rather than attempting to play lightning-fast hammers and pulls on one string, we'll finger these two notes as a harmonic interval and quickly strum them. Sustaining a smooth tremolo for three beats takes practice, so start at a relaxed tempo and slowly work up to speed.

Next time you're comping a slow 12-bar shuffle, substitute this lick for each chord in the progression. For instance, here, we're outlining *G7*. Move to the eighth position for *C7* and the tenth position for *D7*.

Ex. 6

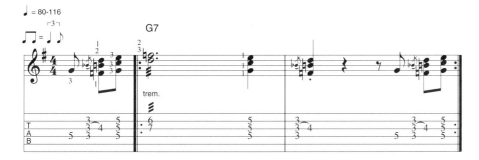

In **Ex. 7**, a lovely I–IV riff distilled from "Blues All Day Long" by Groove Holmes, we start sketching *B♭7* above the *B♭* blues box, drop down into it, and finally emerge below it to catch *E♭9*, the IV chord. What's particularly significant is how bar 1's double-stops all stem from a 1st-finger partial barre. No doubt you've played these notes many times before, but odds are not with this precise fingering. This is a case of sound dictating the moves: We want to slur each interval yet keep them uniform. The best way to accomplish this is to turn our 1st and 2nd fingers into a mobile hammering and pulling machine that moves along the fretboard. We can even use these two digits to fret the final *E♭9*—cool.

Ex. 7

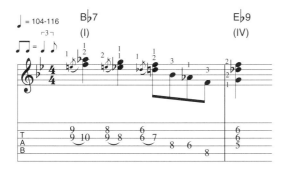

This groovy turnaround (**Ex. 8**) comes courtesy of McDuff by way of Grant Green's "Blues in Maude's Flat." Pop this two-bar phrase into bars 11 and 12 of a blues in *G*, and you'll be smiling.

Like many fine turnarounds, this contains a stepwise line (*F, E, E♭, D, D♭, C*) played against a static tone (*G*). It keeps your 4th finger dancing, so take it slowly at first. By now, you know all about the *G7–C–G7* flourish at the end, right?

Ex. 8

Jimmy McGriff's "I've Got a Woman" is a textbook example of soul-jazz organ moves, and **Ex. 9** contains two of his cool melodic riffs. In the middle of bars 1 and 3, notice how we hold a high note (*C* and *F*, respectively) while playing a descending run that ends with an interval of a minor tenth.

Like most organs used for jazz, the Hammond B-3 boasts two manuals (or keyboards). This allows several slick tricks, one of which is to hold a note with one hand while riffing above or below it with the other. In this example, we mimic the dual-manual sound by sustaining a note with the 4th finger while playing a descending run with the other three. It's subtle but fat.

Ex. 9

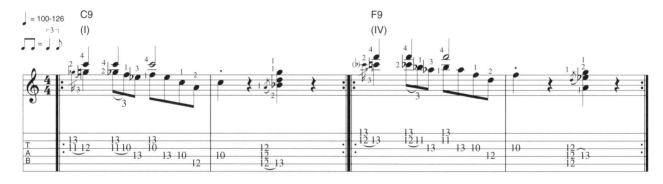

First practice the *C9* and *F9* phrases independently, then comp a 12-bar blues in *C* using these two moves. You've already got the first eight bars covered with the I and IV licks shown here. For the V–IV–I–V shift that occurs in the final four measures of a 12-bar blues, try this:

- To hit bar 9's *G9*, transplant the first measure of *C9*'s phrase to the fifth position (anchor your 4th finger on *G* at the 8th fret).
- Then, for bar 10's *F9*, simply drop the same figure down two frets to the third position.
- Finally, to fill bars 11 and 12, transpose Ex. 8's turnaround from *G* to *C*. This will put you in the eighth position—the *C* blues box—for the concluding fireworks.

Most of our examples are notated with a swing feel for that smoky Blue Note sound. However, in the late '60s and early '70s, soul-jazz embraced boogaloo grooves played with straight eighths and a heavy backbeat. **Ex. 10** gives you an idea of what to play in such settings.

Adapted from funky riffs in McGriff's "Fat Cakes," this four-bar passage features a wicked tritone (*B♭–E* in bar 1). Guitarists tend to bend into this interval (T-Bone Walker and Chuck Berry showed us how), but on the organ, the best you can do is quickly skip from *E♭* to *E♮*. We can imitate this clicky sound by simply hammering from a fourth to a tritone.

That last line on the fifth and fourth strings (from the "and" of beat four, bar 3, through beat three, bar 4) is a funk-jazz mainstay. Use a variation of this sequence whenever a blues-derived riff sounds too raw. The difference? Here, the notes come from a *C* major pentatonic scale (*C–D–E–G–A*, or 1–2–3–5–6), as opposed to a *C* minor pentatonic (*C–E♭–F–G–B♭*, or 1–♭3–4–5–♭7). It all comes down to the sweetness of the 6 versus the tartness of the ♭7.

Ex. 10

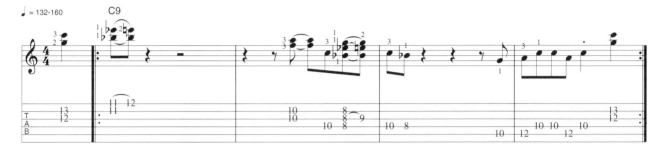

When you want to turn heads, play **Ex. 11**'s lines through a rotary speaker or simulator. To hear Jimmy Smith work these sounds, listen to "Blue Bash," which he recorded with Kenny Burrell. Wow!

The tritones make this figure special. First, we outline the I chord (*C9*) by hammering into *B♭–E* (♭7–3). Then in bar 2 we establish the IV (*F9*) by hammering into *A–E♭* (3–♭7). These moves are only a half-step apart, so the harmony has the closest possible voice leading. Notice how on the fourth string the ♭7 moves to the 3, and how on the third string the 3 shifts to the ♭7. Jazz and R&B horn players use this trick all the time.

If you're looking for the V chord's (*G9*) tritone on the fourth and third strings, just bump the I chord's tritone up a fret to *B–F*. Those hammers work here too. Yup—now you have another way to comp a medium tempo 12-bar blues.

Ex. 11

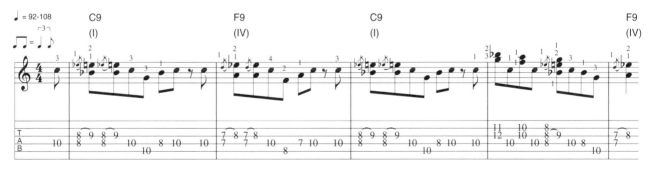

We'll wrap up this faux-organ lesson with a V–IV–I double-stop workout in the key of *A* (**Ex. 12**). Notice how in each measure we perform the same routine—initially on the first and second strings, and then the second and third strings. There are two ways to analyze what we're doing:

- While we hold a high-chord root, we resolve the chord's ♭5 up to the 5 or down to the 4.
- We alternately shrink a diminished fifth to a perfect fourth or expand a diminished fifth to a perfect fifth.

These four measures provide you with all the necessary double-stop mojo to comp an organic shuffle the next time you're performing onstage or at a jam session. Round out the fills with voicings from Examples 1 and 2, and you'll be set.

Ex. 12

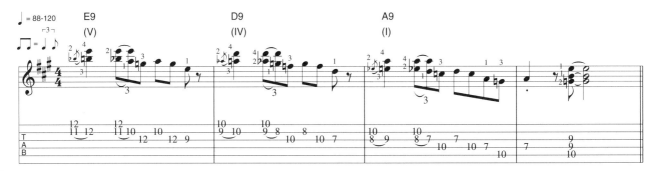

You can—and should—snap apart and recombine all the moves and phrases we've covered in these dozen examples. To comp well, you needn't know 100 different patterns, but rather how to transpose and reconfigure five cool maneuvers in 20 ways. Think of it as musical recycling. If you're crafty, you can create the illusion of having an endless supply of grooves.

To see how the masters play this game, search out *Blue Bash!* by Kenny Burrell and Jimmy Smith, Smith's *Back at the Chicken Shack* (which also includes Burrell), *The Honeydripper* by Jack McDuff (featuring Grant Green), and the excellent two-CD collection *The Blue Note Years, Organ and Soul.* ∎

Bob Brozman

Courtesy Bob Brozman; Photo: Ali Madjdi

Slide Away

Bob Brozman's Bottleneck Breakdown

BY ANDY ELLIS

Some players avoid musical analysis at all costs," says resophonic wizard Bob Brozman. "They say, 'Well, you just break a bottle on the sidewalk and slide its neck around on the strings. If you *think* about it, you kill the music.' I'm sorry, I don't buy that. Thinking about music is just another way to enjoy it. It doesn't kill anything."

Watching Brozman assault one of his vintage National guitars, you'd never guess he delights in analyzing music. The man plays as if possessed: Percussive *braaps* and *thwacks* punctuate edgy melodies as his hands alternately caress and pound the chromed beauty. He'll be thundering along, glass slide whining a melismatic counterpoint to his plaintive vocal holler, and suddenly slam on the brakes to coax swooping harmonics from the guitar's still-shuddering belly. Cradling his axe in a moaning embrace, Bob generates enough energy to power a small trailer park.

When not playing wildman, Brozman is completely lucid—ready, willing, and able to demystify bottleneck technique. He's spent nearly three decades collecting and devouring old 78 RPM records, books, catalogs, photos, and artifacts pertaining

to his passion—early blues and Hawaiian music. Bob is equally comfortable in the role of scholar (his *The History & Artistry of National Resonator Instruments*, published by Centerstream, is *the* definitive book on the subject) as he is rocking a French concert hall. I spent an unforgettable afternoon at his Santa Cruz mountain home, listening to him patiently reveal the secrets of slide guitar.

"Slide is so much more expressive than fretting," Brozman begins. "You can control how wide and fast the vibrato is and the speed at which you arrive at the note." Complex slide technique, he insists, can be broken down into essential gestures and skills. The journey starts with tuning.

Joys of G

Brozman relies on open-*G* tuning—*DGDGBD*, low to high—for most of his slide work (**Ex. 1**).

"I prefer it for two reasons. The beauty note is sliding up *into* the tonic *G* on the first string (**Ex. 2**). A lot of players play in *D* or *E* tuning, but there you're stuck with the tonic as an open string.

Ex. 1   **Ex. 2**

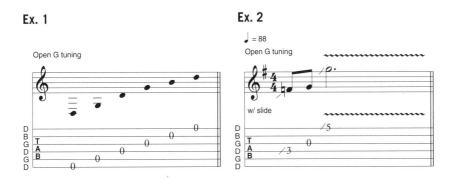

"The top interval is tighter in *G* tuning. It's a minor third (*B–D*, **Ex. 3a**), which sounds more pointy than the fourth you get in open *D* (*A–D*, Ex. **3b**). The minor third is more interesting to me musically. Its blues sound is not as ambiguous as a fourth."

Ex. 3a   **Ex. 3b**

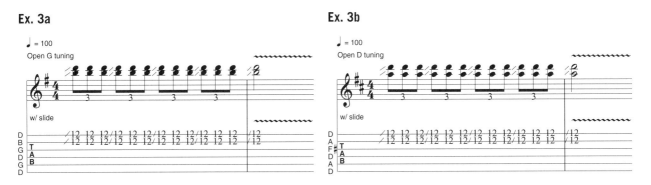

To Brozman, open *G* is the universal tuning that unites guitar music around the world. "In Africa, Mexico, Cuba, South America, and Hawaii, it's the first tuning people came up with. Delta blues tuning is the same as the basic Hawaiian guitar tuning."

He uses heavy phosphor-bronze strings, gauged .059, .049, .039, .028, .018, .016. "I'd use a heavier sixth string if I could find one," he allows. For electric guitar, Bob recommends tuning up a whole-step to increase the tension of lighter strings. Naturally, this open-*A* tuning (*EAEAC♯E*, low to high) maintains the interval relationship of open *G*.

Bob's favorite slide is cut from a pre-1973 Mateus rosé bottle. (Pre-'73 Mateus bottles have a bluish cast to their green tint, Bob notes.) He wears the bottleneck on his pinky, freeing his other fingers to fret notes.

Brozman arches his left-hand fingers over the strings, resting the tip of his ring finger in a small chipped indentation on the slide. His fingertips form a semicircle. "It's like I'm holding a small orange. In fact, *everything* about slide is curved. A lot of slide players play flat, but to me that's like moving a brick up and down the strings. It's not as subtle."

Damping Secrets

Brozman uses both hands for damping. "To get rid of the sound *behind* the slide," he reveals, "I damp the way Tampa Red did, by using the flesh of my index finger to lightly touch the string. All that's required is *contact*, rather than pressure. Same with the slide—contact, not pressure. This gives me three points of left-hand support: thumb, index finger, and slide.

"When you lift the slide from the strings to change hand positions, there's a little buzz. I damp that and all other spurious noises with the right hand." Since Bob wears plastic picks on his right thumb, index, and middle fingers, he can't damp with his bare fingertips the way, say, Duane Allman did. Instead, Brozman damps with his palm. "It's like there's a massive spring always holding my right hand down on the strings. The only thing that releases it is plucking a string. Unless I'm sustaining a note, the 'spring' closes immediately after. If the damping stroke made a sound, it would be a really clipped 16th-note behind the beat."

Scratchin' Dog

Describing his vibrato, Bob says, "When a dog scratches behind his ear, he's not thinking 'scratch, scratch, scratch, scratch,' every time he moves. He just hits a nerve circuit in his brain and goes! It's like that with vibrato. You'll drive yourself nuts if you think 'left-right, left-right, left-right, left-right.' It's more of a *throwing* thing. Imagine a bowl of Jell-O that you're wiggling back and forth. When you've swung the bowl to one side, the Jell-O is still on its way over—it follows your motion. When you're doing vibrato right, you can feel the fat and muscles on the back of your upper arm wiggling that way.

"I divide my whole arm into two parts: Part one is my thumb and the little bit of flesh on my index finger that's damping. That stays still. The Jell-O, part two, is the weight of the slide—that's why I use a heavy glass slide—plus the weight of the rest of my hand and my entire arm. I'm really hanging all this weight off my shoulder." And vibrato width? "Normally, I move a full fret. That's wider than some folks. It's the Hawaiian influence, I guess. Sometimes the rate of vibrato has a musical relation to the beat; sometimes it doesn't."

Key Moves

Brozman adopts a martial arts approach to teaching slide technique, distilling it into a few essential moves that you master individually and then recombine for spontaneous play. "I only use a handful of elements: slides, staccato notes, staccato notes alternating with open strings, long slides into staccato notes, and what I call strike and slide."

The first string is the starting point. "Ninety percent of slide action happens on the top three strings, with the majority occurring on the first." To develop pitch control, run your slide gently up or down the first string, stopping directly over a fret. Listen to the resulting tone. Use your open D (or open lower strings) as a reference to refine your intonation. Pluck, slide, park, and listen. Repeat the process until you can slide into a note with reasonable accuracy from below or above.

"Playing staccato notes with a slide is not obvious," Bob admits, "but it's an essential technique. My basic staccato exercise consists of moving chromatically from, say, the 5th fret to 12th fret (**Ex. 4**). Each time I change a note, I lift the slide, but *not* my damping finger." The index damping finger mutes the buzz caused by the slide contacting the string at the onset of each new note.

Ex. 4

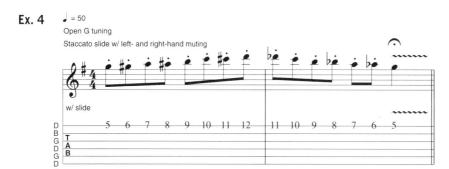

You face a different challenge when you need to play an open string between staccato notes. "Now you have to lift *both* your slide and index damping finger." When you renew contact with the string, the damper lands just ahead of the slide. Take **Ex. 5** slowly at first, until you nail that two-point landing. Keep those fingertips curved—remember the imaginary orange.

Ex. 5

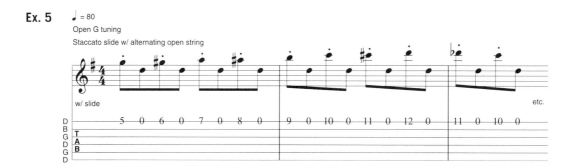

Ex. 6 features long slides that end with a staccato note. Bob recommends this exercise as a way to improve intonation by synchronizing your muscles and ears. "You have to rush up there and then stop *dead* without fishing around for the note. You have to overcome the inertia. This teaches you accuracy—eventually you won't have to look."

Ex. 6

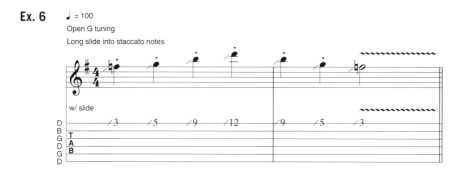

Reverse the exercise and try downward glisses that end with a staccato note. "They're a little harder and more cartoony, but they're good for developing accuracy."

Ex. 7 illustrates the "strike and slide" technique: "I hit a note and then rhythmically slide to another note to get a second pitch." Once you've got the hang of this *G7* arpeggio, apply the technique to different chords.

Ex. 7

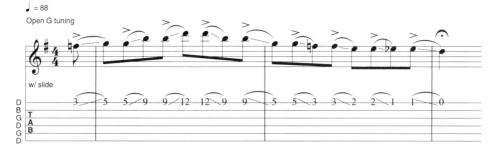

Angle of the Dangle

Ex. 8 provides a musical context for the previous moves and concepts. Play the lick with a relaxed swing feel.

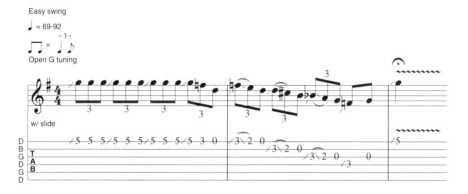

"You'll notice that the last lick moves from the first string down to the fourth," says Bob. "I position my slide differently, according to which strings I'm playing." On the first string, he aims his fingertip skyward, at roughly a 45-degree angle. This outward tilt lets Bob lay the slide on the first string without having the end snag or contact any lower strings. When playing parallel intervals on interior strings, Brozman levels his slide on the strings and wails away. When playing single-note lines on interior strings, he tilts his slide in the opposite direction (fingertip down, hand up), contacting the target string with only the rounded lip of his glass bottleneck. "In this position, I reduce my damping to just the tip of my left index finger on that string." **Ex. 9** contains all three positions, as indicated above the notation.

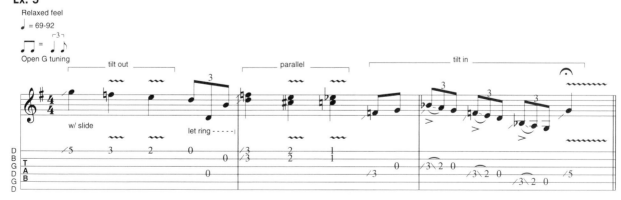

One particular note—B♭ on the third string—is integral to Brozman's slide shows. "I call it 'your buddy,'" he laughs. "Almost every lick bounces off this note, like 'Little Red Rooster,' which Howlin' Wolf stole from Robert Johnson, which Robert Johnson stole from Son House." Dig **Ex. 10**. This riff features "your buddy," a choice gliss into the tonic, and intriguing intervals. The jump at the end is over two octaves. Pay attention to side angle: Tilt *in* on the third string, then *out* on the first.

Ex. 10

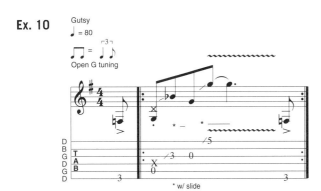

In **Ex. 11**, Bob works the "Little Red Rooster" lick into a hip four-bar phrase. If you've worked diligently on the earlier moves, your reward is to navigate this lick with relative ease. Mind your mutes and slide tilt.

Ex. 11

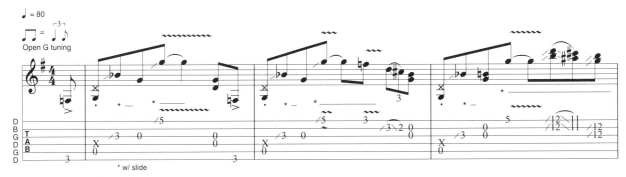

Palm Harmonics

Bob laces his lines with artificial slide harmonics. He generates these tasty morsels by gently brushing the octave node (found exactly 12 frets above where the slide is contacting the string) with the karate-chop edge of his right hand. He picks the strings on the headstock side of the node. "You need a thumbpick to do this right," Bob cautions. Once you've activated the harmonic, you can move the slide, thus changing the pitch of the harmonic at will. "I don't lay my palm on the strings. I strum *through* the harmonics. My point of contact is a single dot on my hand that travels across the strings.

"You can't look at both hands simultaneously when you do palm harmonics—it's impossible. I like to watch my slide hand now and again for intonation, so I've learned to find the node by feel." There's a trick, he concedes. As you slide along the strings, your right hand travels exactly half the distance of your left. "In time you develop an intuitive sense for it." Use **Ex. 12**, with its chromatic open chords, to get a handle on the 2:1 ratio. "Do this until you're bored to death," Bob advises.

Ex. 12

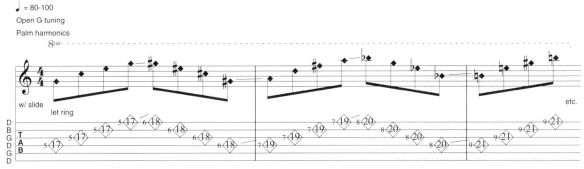

Palm harmonics can add drama to your playing. "The best way to grab an audience is not to get louder but suddenly quieter," Bob says. He suggests working up quick palm flourishes, such as **Ex. 13**, and sprinkling them into longer passages.

"The super-advanced version of this, which the greatest Hawaiian guys did so well, is to play harmonics up to—but *not* including—the top string." **Ex. 14** illustrates the technique. Played as harmonics, lower-string arpeggios become transparent; any top-string melody gets emphasized accordingly. Notice that with palm harmonics the interval in beat three gets inverted, changing from a fifth to a fourth. Once you master this mixed harmonic-and-note trick, you'll be able to voice chords that are impossible to play using conventional slide technique. It's worth a good, oh, five years of study.

Ex. 13

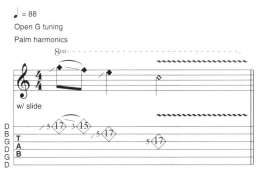

Ex. 14

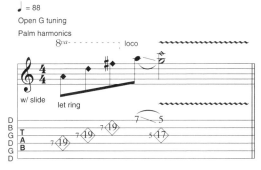

Like so many great players, Brozman is quick to emphasize that creative freedom lies in learning skills, not licks. "Take these principles and apply them in as many ways as you can. Experiment. That's how you develop your own voice." ■

Slide in Standard Tuning

Muddy Waters, late '60s

BY ARLEN ROTH

Many people start playing standard-tuning slide without realizing that the sounds they are trying to emulate were created in open tunings by traditional slide players such as Elmore James, Robert Johnson, and Tampa Red. Some guitarists even try to play the sounds with a pick, even though fingerpicking is best for any kind of slide work—damping and muting become so much easier with it.

When I shot a video with former Bluesbreaker/Rolling Stone Mick Taylor, I was astounded by the clean sound he got playing slide with a pick and in standard tuning. The only problem is that this method creates a sound closer to regular fretted notes—the extreme damping required makes things sound staccato. Nevertheless, it's important for you to develop a slide technique, and the big advantage of standard-tuning slide is that you can add it to your bag of tricks without having to change guitars or retune. (Muddy Waters was among those who enjoyed that convenience.)

Standard-tuning slide has far fewer harmony-note possibilities than, say, open-*E* tuning. In open tunings, your chord positions reach across all six strings, but in standard tuning, the only available major chord occurs across the *D, G,* and *B* strings.

It's around this position that the box pattern [see "Tale of the Scale," page 1] lies, with the most opportunities for soloing. In the key of *E*, for example, this is at the 9th fret, while in open-*E* tuning it involves all the strings at the 12th fret. Consider the blues scale that starts at the 12th fret on the high *E*-string and ends at the 12th fret on the low *E*-string in open-*E* tuning. To play in standard tuning you have to travel from the same starting point all the way to the 7th fret on the *A* string! If you don't damp at all, the open-tuning version at least sounds like an *E* chord, while the standard-tuning version is a dissonant blur.

You should hold the slide on your little finger—try to get a slide that allows your finger *just* enough exposure at the end so you can "sense" the end of the slide (and, therefore, the string you're playing). It's also important to keep the slide at a right angle to the strings and to only cover the strings that are necessary. This helps damping quite a bit and eliminates a lot of unwanted noise. Here are some of my favorite standard-tuning slide licks (**Examples 1–6**).

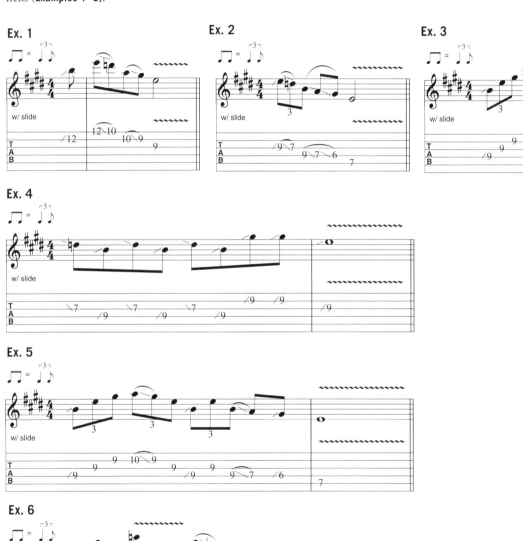

Even though standard-tuning slide isn't traditional, there are certain licks and positions that are common to both standard tuning and the more versatile open tunings. Keep in mind that proper blocking and damping are essential for a clean sound in standard-tuning slide, because you don't have all those nice chords and harmonies to fall back on.

I like using open-position licks for slide guitar, and standard tuning is no exception. A few nice harmony positions do exist in standard tuning, but when it comes to playing standard-sounding blues licks, you'll have to follow the notes as you do when playing regular lead guitar, using some very critical and deft left- and right-hand damping. **Examples 7–13** show just what I'm talking about. The first four use open-string notes as melody notes or harmonies, while the last three are very much like "closed"-position blues licks, but played with a slide rather than fingers. **Examples 11–13** also show the difficult technique of using standard-tuning slide to simulate regular lead playing. Have fun, and experiment as much as possible with this challenging technique. ■

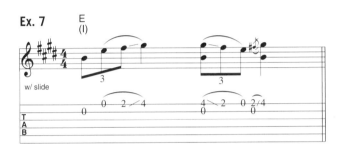

B.B. King and Eric
Clapton, late '60s

Two Kings

Nine Magical Blues Licks from Clapton & B.B.

BY ADAM LEVY

E ric Clapton and B.B. King—two of the most exciting and original guitarists to play the blues—have instantly recognizable sounds. Is this because of their tone? Their phrasing? Their touch? Yes, yes, and yes! These, and many less-tangible clues, tell us whom we're hearing.

Like most of us, King and Clapton started by copying their heroes. For King, the list included T-Bone Walker, Lonnie Johnson, and Blind Lemon Jefferson. Clapton was inspired by Otis Rush, Buddy Guy, and the three Kings—Freddie, B.B., and Albert. Eventually, King and Clapton transformed their hero worship into the unique styles we now know and love. But how and when did the Jell-O set in its mold? The best way to answer these questions is to revisit early and mid-period recordings by King and Clapton, and observe how each guitarist spun new fabric from the threads of their forebears.

Blues à la King

In the mid-1950s, King was under the spell of T-Bone Walker, who blended jazz, R&B, and jump blues into a refined, modern hybrid. **Ex. 1**, a hip turnaround lick,

shows the kind of jazzy lines that were part of King's Walker-inspired vocabulary at the time. Note the chromatic descent from *E* to *D* in bar 1 and the descending *D* and *D♭* triad shapes in bar 2 (beats one through three). The dissonant *D♭* triad eventually works its way down to a *C* triad (the first three eighth-notes of bar 3) before outlining the tonic *G* chord with *B* and *D*—its 3 and 5.

Ex. 1

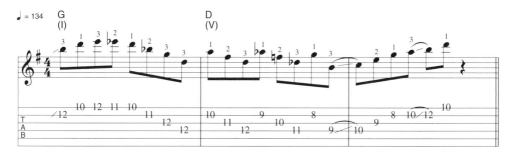

Among King enthusiasts, there is little debate that *Live at the Regal* is one of his finest works—and one of the classic live records. Recorded in 1964, the album captures King holding court at Chicago's Regal Theater, backed by a tight six-man ensemble. We hear how he could work an audience of young fans into an ecstatic frenzy with his combination of crafty showmanship, emotive guitar, and honey-toned vocals.

One of the most precious jewels in *Live at the Regal*'s crown is "Sweet Little Angel"—a King original and a staple of his '50s and '60s live shows. His performance is full of choice licks, and **Ex. 2** offers a sweet taste of slow-blues sugar. Bar 2's final *G, C, G, C, C* cadence is a patented King move—particularly the repeated *C* at the end of the line, played on the first and second strings, respectively. You can fret the final *C* with your 3rd or 4th finger, and you can either hit the note straight on or slide into it from a half-step below for a King-sanctioned variation.

Ex. 2

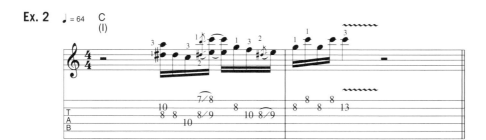

King followed *Live at the Regal* with a string of sparkling releases, but his next big record was 1969's *Completely Well*, which featured his career-making crossover hit, "The Thrill Is Gone." This is where we really begin to see King move beyond his '50s jump-blues roots and into his own style. Although the moody, minor-key "Thrill" contains schmaltzy overdubbed violins, most of the album features a revved-up King and raw, meaty tones.

Based on some of King's *Completely Well* ideas, **Ex. 3** offers a stirring route from I to IV (a progression found in the fourth and fifth bars of a typical 12-bar blues). Notice how the tension builds in bar 1 with the use of upbeats (the "and" of beats one and two) and a blustery hammer/pull move (beat four). The rhythmic tension then releases in bars 2 and 3, where there is relatively little activity. Bar 2 has another kind of tension, however, as you gradually bend *B* ("and" of beat two) up to *D*. Your audience should wonder, "Wow—are you going to make it?"

Ex. 3

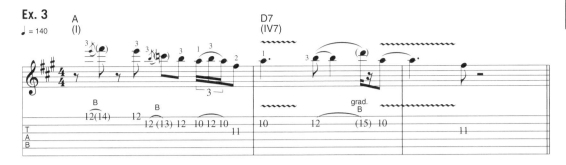

In the '70s and early '80s, King's albums such as *To Know You Is to Love You* and *Midnight Believer* presented his vocals as the main attraction, and his guitar tones tended to be a little thinner and less present in the mix. But in 1988 King teamed up with U2 and producer Jimmy Iovine to record "When Love Comes to Town" on *Rattle and Hum*. This song bares the brashest tones King's fans had heard in a long while.

His lead breaks on "When Love Comes to Town" are righteous, matching U2's fiery energy blow for blow. Drawn from King's ideas, **Ex. 4** demonstrates the action. This four-bar phrase begins with an attention-getting *E* minor pentatonic burst. King brightens the minor mood by following the descending five-note run with *C♯*—a note in the *E* major pentatonic scale.

Ex. 4

Again, King emphasizes upbeats to add tension to the melodic line. Here's how:
- By starting on the last eighth-note of bar 1, he anticipates the first note of bar 2.
- The *G♮* on the "and" of beat two adds more upbeat momentum.
- The final bent *B* ("and" of beat four) finishes the bar on an upbeat.

Set between the decidedly unsyncopated bar 1 and the even more square bar 3, the upbeat-heavy bar 2 perfectly balances the phrase's overall feel. King is a master of such controlled tension—one of the skills that separates the men from the boys in blues.

Slowhand's Blues Power

While Eric Clapton's work in the Yardbirds is noteworthy, it wasn't until he left the 'Birds' nest and joined John Mayall's Bluesbreakers that he came into his own as a heavyweight blues champion. **Ex. 5**—a I–IV–I phrase inspired by Clapton's Bluesbreaker-era lines—illustrates how the young Slowhand was already cocksure enough to take his time with a solo. Note the use of sustained notes in each bar, which give the phrase a composed—in both senses of the word—vibe. Also notice how bar 2's downbeat *D* is set up by a descending triplet (*C♮*, *A*, *E*) on beat four of bar 1, and how bar 3's *A7* is anticipated by bar 2's two final notes (*C♯*, *A*). Such anticipations can keep a solo rolling.

After leaving the Bluesbreakers in July '66, Clapton formed Cream with drummer Ginger Baker and bassist Jack Bruce. While the guitarist's musical heart and soul still belonged to the blues, Baker and Bruce shared a penchant for a wild, polyrhythmic, electrified breed of jazz. The fusion of these elements made Cream unique and gave Clapton a new context in which to work his blues mojo.

Ex. 5

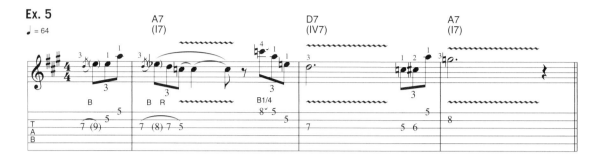

There are several Old School blues numbers on *Fresh Cream*—the band's 1966 debut—including Willie Dixon's "Spoonful" and Skip James's "I'm So Glad." But the record's most down and dirty cut is the Bruce original, "Sleepy Time Time." The slow 12-bar blues offers a golden opportunity for Clapton to burn, and he does just that. **Ex. 6** is a I–IV–I–V7 turnaround lick in the spirit of E.C.'s "Sleepy Time Time" moves.

Disraeli Gears, the follow-up to *Fresh Cream*, found the band stepping into psychedelic territory, with more adventurous songwriting and wilder tones—including Clapton's first recorded use of a wah pedal. Still, his blues roots were evident on such cuts as "Strange Brew" (on which E.C. borrows liberally from Albert King's "Oh, Pretty Woman" solo) and "Sunshine of Your Love." Of course, a big part of Clapton's magic is that when he cops licks from other players, his phrasing and dynamics make the lines his own. (As Clapton noted in the July '95 *Guitar Player*, "I'll start with a Freddie King line and then go to a B.B. King line. I'll do something to join them up, so that part will be me.")

Derived from Clapton's "Strange Brew" solo, **Ex. 7** shows an archetypal Slowhand move in which you deftly pivot between the eighth-position and fifth-position *A* minor pentatonic boxes. The pivot point is the third-string slide down from the 9th fret to 7th fret (bar 2, beat three). Simply reverse the maneuver to shift back up (bar 3, "and" of four).

Ex. 6

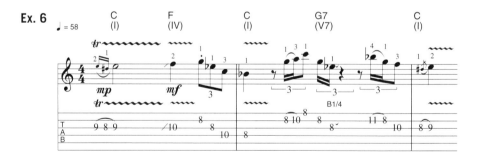

Ex. 7

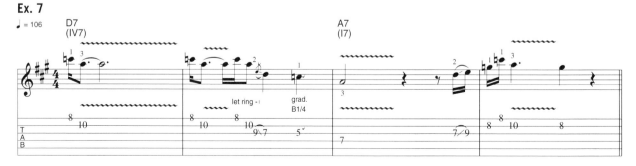

The King's English

To add an authentic, singing sound to the B.B. King licks in this lesson, you'll need to enhance your notes with a touch of his "hummingbird" vibrato. Try this: With your fretting-hand elbow loosely planted at your side, extend your hand and gently curl your fingers, as if reaching for a doorknob. Next, jiggle the imaginary doorknob, using a rotary motion that causes your palm to alternately face up and down. This alternating motion is very quick, and should occur entirely in your forearm—not your elbow or shoulder.

Now it's time to try this with guitar in hand. Plant your 1st finger on E (third string, 9th fret).

With your metronome or drum machine set at a comfortable "walking" tempo (about 90 BPM), hit the E and jiggle the doorknob. Practice this move on the second-string E (at the 5th fret), and then do the doorknob dance with different notes. You can add this sting to the tonic note of whatever key you're in.

One more point: If you have a metronome going, you've probably been hitting your E's smack on the downbeat. That's fine, but King will just as often sting an upbeat—such as the "and" of beat two or four—to give his line a subtle rhythmic push.

In 1970 Clapton rode yet another musical wave with Derek & The Dominos. Recruiting bottleneck ace Duane Allman, Clapton created the masterpiece *Layla & Other Assorted Love Songs* with tunes such as "Layla," "Bell Bottom Blues," and "Why Does Love Got to Be So Sad?" *Layla* showed a mellower side of Clapton, and the songs had little to do with the blues. But even without a 12-bar, I–IV–V backdrop, Slowhand couldn't help but imbue his lines with a sad soulfulness. **Ex. 8**, an *A* minor pentatonic lick evocative of Clapton's *Layla*-era playing, suggests this reflective side. The faux pedal-steel move (bar 1, beat three) plays up the lick's slightly country flavor. Make sure to hold the bent *E* ("and" of beat two) when you strike the high *G*, so that you have, in effect, a released bend on the second 16th-note of beat three.

Ex. 8

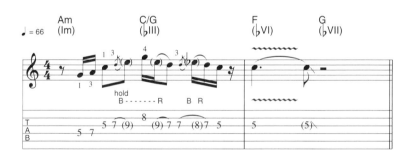

With such records as *461 Ocean Boulevard*, *Another Ticket*, *Money and Cigarettes*, and *Behind the Sun*, Clapton spent much of the late 1970s and '80s positioning himself as a singer and songwriter, and it seemed he had hung up his "guitar hero" hat for good. But in 1994 Clapton released *From the Cradle*—a collection of classic tunes by Lowell Fulson, Willie Dixon, Muddy Waters, Elmore James, and Freddie King. The record is much more than a salute to Clapton's predecessors—it's a full-blown bluesfest, with riveting vocal performances and some of the baddest guitar he has ever recorded.

Ex. 9 is in the same mood as Clapton's soloing on some of *Cradle*'s slow blues tracks, such as "Third Degree," "Reconsider Baby," and "Someday After a While." With its opening triplet, this phrase is a variation of one of the prime blues licks of all time. The lick is generally attributed to T-Bone Walker, who used it on his early-'40s recording of "Stormy Monday." It's hard to overstate Walker's impact on blues guitarists. As B.B. King himself explained in the March '75 *Guitar Player*, "I can still hear T-Bone in my mind today from that first record I heard—'Stormy Monday.' He was the first electric guitar player I heard on record. He made me know I just had to go out and get an electric guitar."

For a jazzy, Walker-esque twist, replace the ♭3 (*B♭*, first string, 6th fret), with the 9 (*A*, a half-step lower, at the 5th fret).

Ex. 9

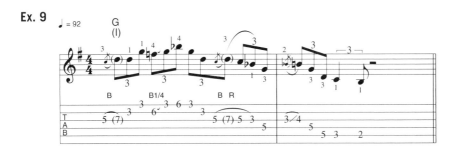

The lick works nicely as an intro or turnaround, and can be very effective in bars 6 and 7 of a 12-bar blues in *G*—in which case the chords would be *C* (or *C7*) for the first bar of the lick, and *G* (or *G7*) for the second bar. Here's why this lick sits so nicely at that point in a 12-bar progression: The *B♭*s refer to *C7* (they're the chord's ♭7) and the *B♮*s (the ♮3) harmonize with *G* or *G7*.

Beyond the Crossroads

"There's nothing wrong with trying to play like someone—in the beginning," counseled B.B. King in the September '93 *Guitar Player*. "But then as you learn, you start to think that there's already one of them. So you try to play as you play." In other words, once you've got these King- and Clapton-style licks under your belt, it's your duty to make them your own. How? Try these tips for extra-credit blues homework:

• Using each of these phrases as a template, craft new licks by slightly varying the rhythms and note choices. Each lick can spawn scores of variations.

• The tempo markings are given to indicate the tempo at which Clapton or King might play each respective lick, but you can personalize the lines by trying them at a variety of tempos—from dirge to walking pace to sprint.

• Try playing some of these licks an octave higher or lower than written. Recasting them up or down an octave can give them a new spin, while keeping their musical conception intact. (And while you're at it, try transposing them to other keys. Sometimes just moving a lick up or down a few frets lets you hear it from a different perspective.)

• Listen to recordings of King and Clapton without trying to dissect their lines note for note. Try to tune into the essence of their phrases without literally walking in the kings' footsteps. ◼

Howlin' Wolf,
early '70s

Michael Ochs Archives.Com

Fathers & Sons

The London-Chicago Blues Connection

BY ANDY ELLIS

In the mid '60s, restless British musicians, bored with folky skiffle and sugary radio fare, found inspiration in late-'50s and early-'60s electric blues. No sappiness here: This gritty, pulsing music dealt with reality—the pain and pleasure of urban life from an African-American perspective. Borrowing songs by Willie Dixon, Howlin' Wolf, Muddy Waters, John Lee Hooker, and Jimmy Reed, and copping urgent licks and riffs from the three Kings—B.B., Albert, and Freddie—as well as Otis Rush, Buddy Guy, and Hubert Sumlin, the Brits gave the blues a new, high-energy sound. Armed with bigger amps and unabashed enthusiasm, bands such as the Yardbirds and Bluesbreakers rocked dank clubs packed with boisterous London youth who got off on wailing guitar solos.

In this lesson we'll revisit some of the classic riffs, cool turnarounds, and stinging licks that defined the era. This material isn't simply historical. As the Brits did 30 years ago, you can tweak each phrase to suit your style and slip it into blues, R&B, rootsy rock—even swampy country—at your next gig or jam.

FREE Audio Version Online
www.PlayBlues.TrueFire.com

A Pair of Yardbirds

In December '65, the Yardbirds recorded Howlin' Wolf's "Smokestack Lightning" at the BBC studios. Jeff Beck, who that March had replaced Eric Clapton as lead guitarist, played this riff with a biting Tele tone (**Ex. 1a**). Think James Burton meets Hubert Sumlin. The Yardbirds would often turn "Smokestack Lightning" into an extended 15-minute rave-up. In the BBC version (from *Yardbirds ... On Air*), the bass pumps the riff that Jimmy Page would clone three years later to power Led Zeppelin's "How Many More Times." Palm-mute the low *E*, and let the first three notes in bar 2 ring against each other.

For a nastier "Smokestack Lightning" riff, substitute **Ex. 1b** for the first bar of Ex. 1a. The physical difference is subtle—a *C♯* replaces the *D♮* in the double-stop. Instead of adding vibrato, make the resulting tritone (*C♯–G*) howl with a slow quarter-bend.

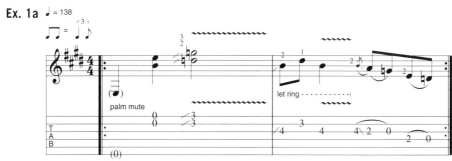

In '65, accompanied only by Jimmy Page chonking out a boogie-woogie rhythm, Eric Clapton recorded several guitar instrumentals. Using a throaty tone and slapback echo, Clapton laid out all the licks that would soon immortalize him in John Mayall's Bluesbreakers. **Ex. 2**'s I7–IV7–I7–V7 turnaround recalls "Freight Loader" from *British Rock Legends*. The quarter-bend in bar 1 is tricky, because it's quickly followed by a lower note on the same string. Quarter-bends, minor-to-major hammers, and quick slides permeate Clapton's playing during these years. Notice how skillfully he weaves chord tones into the line at each change. The *E♭*-to-*E♮* shift (from *F9*'s ♭7 to *C7*'s 3) spanning bars 1 and 2 is particularly sly. The quarter-bend in the concluding double-stop occurs on the third string only. Fret both *G* and *E♭* with your first finger, and gently pull *E♭* toward the floor while holding *G* more or less stationary.

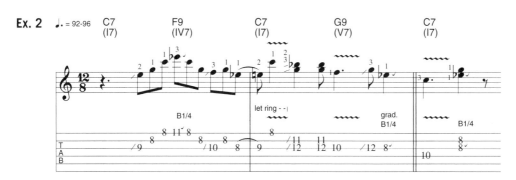

One Tough Bluesbreaker

Mick Taylor was a teenager in June '67 when he replaced Peter Green in Mayall's Bluesbreakers. With his snarling, supple licks on *Crusade*, Taylor quickly proved he had the requisite tone, feel, and chops for the gig. In Albert King's "Oh, Pretty Woman," Taylor played the signature riff with a juicy, sustainy Les Paul tone worthy of his predecessor (**Ex. 3**). Pay attention to the A♮ quarter-bends—the ♭3-verging-on-♮3 is crucial to the British sound. So are the grace-note scrapes in bar 2; downstroke across three consecutive strings as marked. Taylor's vibrato was a tad slower than either Green's or Clapton's, so lay back on those F♯ wiggles.

Ex. 3

While Mick Taylor modeled his "Oh, Pretty Woman" solo after Albert King's (which Clapton would later lift note for note in Cream's "Strange Brew"), Taylor added hot-rod double-stops—a sound not associated with the Flying V–wielding King—as in **Ex. 4**. The trick is to hold the top note on the first string while bending a whole-step against it on the second string at the same fret. (Tip: Bend with your 3rd finger, supported by your 2nd and 1st.) Memorize this crying interval in all keys. The top note is always the key's ♭7, and the bend moves from the 4 to the 5 (B–C♯), offering lots of potential for working through and around the ♭5 (C♮). In this lick, milk the slow release across the bar line for all it's worth.

Ex. 4

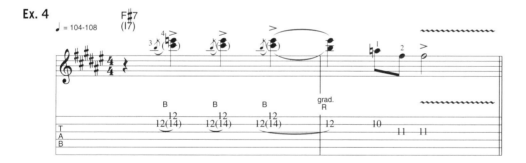

On *Crusade* the Bluesbreakers covered Willie Dixon's "I Can't Quit You Baby," and Taylor's feedback-drenched licks provided the fretboard fire Mayall's fans craved. In the second round of Taylor's extended solo, he grabs the same double-stop/bend we explored in Ex. 4 and pounds it into a 12/8 framework for an intense IV7–I7 transition (**Ex. 5**). This time the releases drop only a half-step, shifting from the IV chord's 9 to the ♭9 (E–E♭) in quick succession. The same stuttering move occurs 12 times in one measure—play it with conviction and a white-hot tone. Remember: In the '60s, amps had no gain knobs or preamp volume control. Distortion was derived from overdriven power tubes, saturated transformers, and speaker breakup. By today's standards, distortion was cleaner and more dynamic. For authentic London-blues tone, dial your preamp gain back and lean harder on the master volume.

Ex. 5

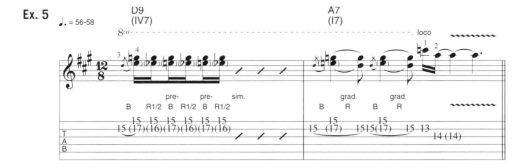

A Page from Zeppelin

Led Zeppelin taped Dixon's "I Can't Quit You Baby" twice for the BBC (*Led Zeppelin, BBC Sessions*). Both versions were heavier and more psychedelic than Mayall's rendition. Derived from a June '69 recording, **Ex. 6a** shows how Page used tension and release to nail a I7–IV7 change. Against *A7*, he crams seven notes into beat four (tension) and then slides into D9's 3—the *F#* (release)—sustaining the note with a slow, wide vibrato.

Page wasn't opposed to inserting country tonalities into his blues, as evidenced by this I7–V7 transition inspired by "I Can't Quit You Baby" (**Ex. 6b**). Ready for a fast, twangy *E* pentatonic lick against *A7*? This dominant chord calls for a *G♮* (A7's ♭7), yet the held *G#* bend sets up an unexpected major 7. It sounds cool—so much for rules. For a truck-driving whine, sustain the notes on all three strings until the final *E*. This bend-one-string-while-holding-two is an essential country maneuver.

Ex. 6a   **Ex. 6b**

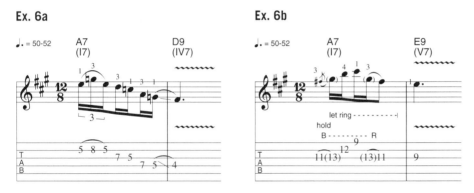

We've seen how Mick Taylor jabbed stuttering double-stop bends into his "I Can't Quit You Baby" solo. Page liked this move, too. Same song, same key, but this time the action spans a V7–IV7 change (**Ex. 6c**). Remember to support the bend with several fingers as you push against *E9* and *D9*.

Ex. 6c

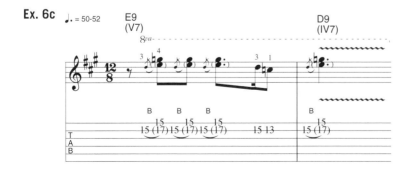

Free's molten-toned Paul Kossoff uses a double-stop blues bend in a rowdy live version of Albert King's "The Hunter" (*Best of Free*). As in **Ex. 6d**, Kossoff sustains the interval for two beats while adding wicked vibrato to the whole-step stretch. Tip: While you bend to *E* and wiggle it, don't let the *G* creep up in pitch. This takes patience; listen to early Kossoff for inspiration.

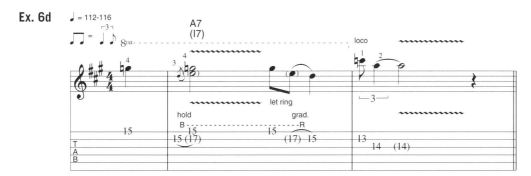

A Bite of Big Mac

Sometimes young British players trekked stateside to record with their blues idols. *Fleetwood Mac in Chicago 1969* documents such an event. Peter Green, Danny Kirwin, and the rest of the original Mac journeyed to Chicago's Chess studio—home of countless classic blues sessions—to cut a double album with Otis Spann, Willie Dixon, Buddy Guy, and other blues greats. Playing for the masters, Green was in particularly fine form. "Watch Out," a medium shuffle, is full of fat-toned, B.B. King–inspired licks. **Ex. 7**'s I7–V7–IV7–I7 phrase illustrates how Green sweated the details: Watch the chromatic slides and quarter-bend. The tangy *C♮* against *E9* is particularly cool; it's one of Green's signature sounds.

In this "Watch Out" lick (**Ex. 8**), Green superimposes a *D* arpeggio against an *A7* chord (beat two) before working the minor/major axis by stretching the *C♮* halfway to *C♯*. This I7 lick also sounds great going from *D9* to *A7*—a IV7–I7 change. Play this with a fat, squawking humbucker tone. (Tip: Be sure to try your favorite licks in several contexts. A familiar melodic line can sound fresh against a new background harmony.)

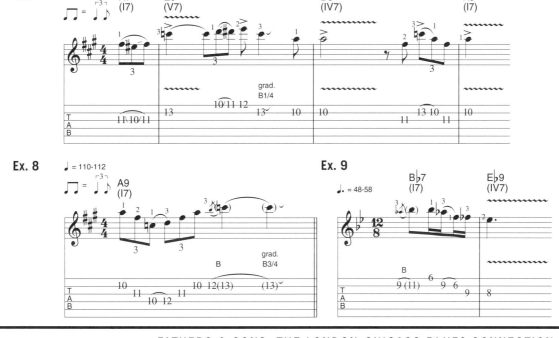

Immediately after recording in Chicago, Peter Green, Danny Kirwin, and Fleetwood Mac bassist John McVie joined Otis Spann and his drummer in a New York studio. This one-day session yielded *The Biggest Thing Since Colossus*, an album brimming with great guitar. Green shines in "Temperature Is Rising (100.2F)"—a slow 12/8 B♭ blues—with licks like this one (**Ex. 9**). The action lies in the chromatic descent into E♭9 via F♭, the ♭5. Add quivering, sweet vibrato to the last note.

"Dig You," an instrumental from *The Biggest Thing Since Colossus*, gave Green and Kirwin a chance to drape their trademark harmony lines over a rumbling blues-piano groove. The bottom part is Green's main riff, Kirwin's major-3rd harmony is shown above. **Ex. 10a** works with *E7*; **Ex. 10b** covers *A7*—the IV7. To hear the effect, first record the lower riffs and then play the harmony along with them. In each part, be sure to add plenty of vibrato to the "and" of beat two. Notice how the E7 riff's lower voice contains G♮, yet the harmony has a G♯. Likewise, the A7 riff has C♮ in the bottom and a C♯ in the top.

Ex. 10c is the V7–IV7–I7 twin-guitar harmony for "Dig You." Keep the vibrato strong on those syncopated beats. In each of these "Dig You" parts, the second guitar joins the main riff on beat two. The lesson? You don't need to harmonize every note.

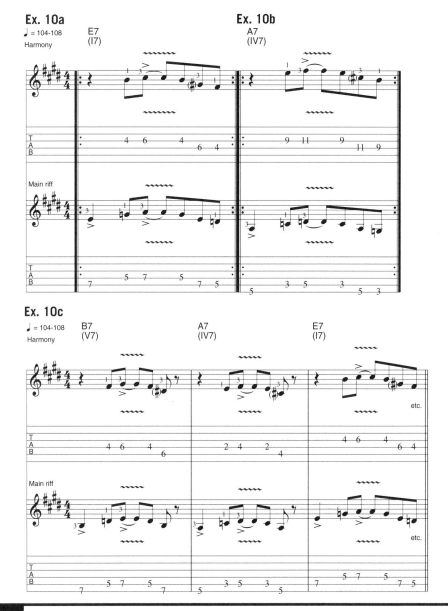

Ex. 10a

Ex. 10b

Ex. 10c

Green shines throughout Spann's *The Biggest Thing Since Colossus*. This lick from "No More Doggin'" features rhythmic variation and a cool half-step bend against a sustained string (**Ex. 11**). Like the whole-step crunch we tackled earlier, this move is transposable, so plug it into all your favorite keys. The top note is always the 5 (*D*); the bend shifts from the ♭3 to the ♮3 (*B♭–B♮*), morphing from a minor to a major tonality. Think open-tuned slide guitar. Play this lick aggressively, use a pulpy tone, and don't rush those quarter-note triplets.

Ex. 11

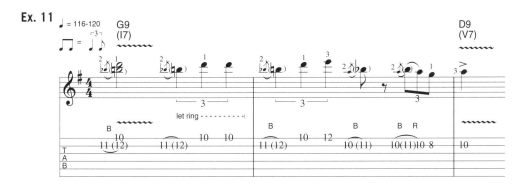

Another nugget from *Colossus*: Full of squalling, belly-toned Les Paul licks, "Someday Baby" is textbook Peter Green. **Ex. 12a** shows how he balanced sustained tones with melodic activity. Really shake the double-stop and give it full value.

Some of the coolest Green licks aren't particularly difficult to fret. In this *A7* treat from "Someday Baby" (**Ex. 12b**), the target note is the ♭7—*G♮*. Before nailing it with a fast wiggle, Green tags virtually every other note in the *A* blues scale.

Ex. 12a

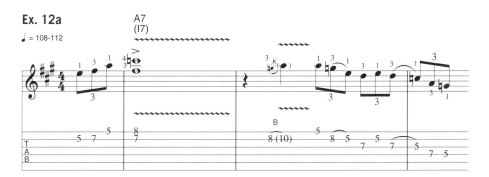

Ex. 12b

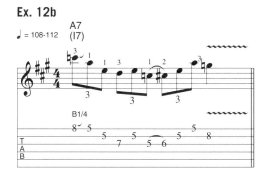

London Calling

When American blues greats toured England, they often made records with a British rhythm section. In 1970 an all-star cast of British rockers backed Howlin' Wolf in the studio. Clapton played lead, while Hubert Sumlin, Wolf's longtime guitarist, played rhythm. In "Sittin' on Top of the World" (*Howlin' Wolf, The London Sessions*), Clapton delivered an *E* turnaround with a grainy, stinging Strat tone (**Ex. 13**). Let the notes in the *B7* arpeggio ring as you move across the strings.

Ex. 13

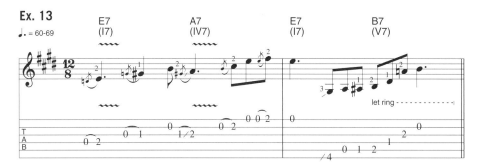

Muddy Waters recorded his "London" album in 1971. Like Wolf, Waters was paired with top rockers for the gig, including Irishman Rory Gallagher and his beat-up sunburst Strat. On "I'm Gonna Move to the Outskirts of Town" (from *Muddy Waters, The London Sessions*), Gallagher used a sweet, clean tone and a heap of smooth whammy vibrato for a surprisingly Hawaiian vibe. Here's one of his turnarounds—a ringing *E*-major pentatonic phrase (**Ex. 14**). Notice how the open strings in bar 1 facilitate the big position change. Compare this to the previous Clapton turnaround: same chords and time signature, and essentially the same tempo. One turnaround ascends, the other descends. Clapton's is bluesier, but also leans heavily on *E* pentatonic tones. The big difference is Clapton's hand vibrato versus Gallagher's lap-steel-inspired trem work.

Ex. 14

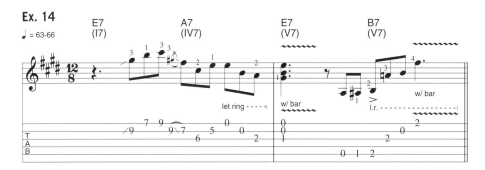

As we've seen, the Brits had a knack for spinning classic blues and R&B riffs into gold. In 1971, Savoy Brown's Kim Simmonds fused Chuck Berry's chunka-chunka rhythm figure with a Robert Johnson turnaround to forge the hook for "Tell Mama," from *Street Corner Talking*. In **Ex. 15a**, the slide (bar 1, beat three) and quarter-bend (bar 2, beat four) put a new twist on Berry's "Roll Over Beethoven" groove.

Robert Johnson through a Marshall? Clapton did it, Page did it. Now you try it—the turnaround to "Tell Mama" (**Ex. 15b**). The final 6/4 bar gives the phrase an elliptical roll. **Ex. 15c** is the classic blues turnaround that Kim Simmonds reworked for "Tell Mama."

Ex. 15a

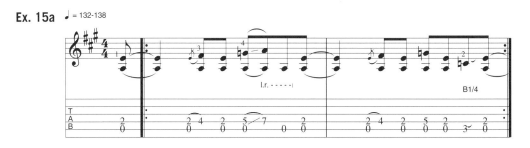

Ex. 15b

Ex. 15c

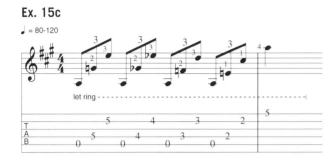

In Chicago in 1960, accompanied by Otis Spann, Hubert Sumlin, and Willie Dixon, Howlin' Wolf recorded Dixon's "Wang Dang Doodle" with a spirited two-beat feel. When Savoy Brown tracked the song 11 years later for *Street Corner Talking*, they built their arrangement around a slinky two-bar riff (**Ex. 16a**). It's great for extended jamming—a must for your collection. Note the minor-major shift (C♮ to C♯, bar 1, beat three). Feel how bar 2's hesitating syncopation pulls you back to the top again? Try a clanky Strat tone.

In Savoy's "Wang Dang Doodle," an electric piano floats the *Am* voicing in **Ex. 16b** above the guitar riff, heightening harmonic interest. After the guitar and bass hammer into C♯ in bar 1, we hear *Am*'s C♮ in bar 2. More of that nebulous major/minor exchange that's at the heart of British blues.

Ex. 16a

Ex. 16b

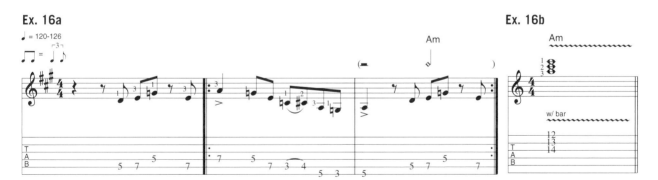

From Memphis to San Francisco

Freddie King recorded Don Nix's "Going Down" in Chicago in 1970. Two years later Jeff Beck made a pilgrimage to Memphis to record *The Jeff Beck Group*. Steve Cropper produced the album, which features a souped-up version of Nix's song. ("Going Down" is included on the *Beckology* box set.) Freddie let the rhythm section handle the riff on his record, opting to fill the cracks with squawky licks. By contrast, Beck careened between riffs and fills. **Ex. 17a** illustrates his take on the signature line. Bar 3's sliding 6ths (*E*) and tritone horn stabs (*F♮–B, E–A♯*) are typical of the flourishes Beck rammed into the track.

Ex. 17a

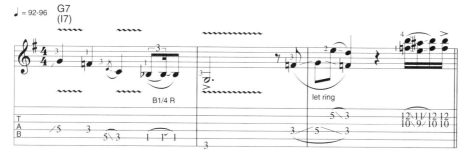

In one of several hair-raising "Going Down" solos, Beck plays a line composed of harmonics to lead from *G7* (I7) to *C9* (IV7). **Ex. 17b**'s *G* major pentatonic (*G, A, B, D, E*) lick rubs nicely against *B♭*s and *F♮*s in the bluesy riff and dominant piano chords churning below. Wait—what's that sneaky fretted note doing in there? With an *A♯* (enharmonically *B♭*—*G7*'s ♭3), Beck drips a dab of blue onto his chimey run. Let the high *B♮* sustain into *C9* (with its *B♭*) for extra dissonance.

Ex. 17b

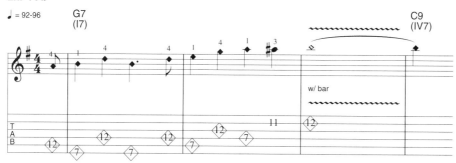

We usually associate Clapton and "Crossroads" with Cream, an SG Les Paul, and a wall of Marshalls. In 1970, however, two years after his ripping performance at San Francisco's Fillmore West, Slowhand recorded a longer, funkier version of Robert Johnson's epic, this time with Derek & The Dominos at New York's Fillmore East (*Live at the Fillmore*). Picking a Strat through smaller amps, Clapton came up with **Ex. 18**. Bar 1 is the song's quasi-country intro that leads the band into the one-measure, palm-muted riff. Also try this on a resonator guitar. ■

Ex. 18

John Lee Hooker,
late '60s

Born to Boogie

An In-Depth Lesson with John Lee Hooker

BY ANDY ELLIS

Let's be real: Trying to imitate John Lee hooker is futile. We've heard credible B.B. King, Albert King, and Eric Clapton knock-offs, but John Lee? Nah. He's simply too unpredictable, too cagey. That's not to say, however, we can't learn from his playing. Hooker's big, bad boogie thrives in the fertile soil of blues-rock—just listen to ZZ Top or Canned Heat. Even artists as diverse as Steely Dan ("Black Friday") and Stevie Wonder ("Higher Ground") draw inspiration from the funky John Lee.

To get a handle on Hooker's churning boogie, you need to listen carefully and master a few basics—keeping time, for starters. John Lee marks time with both feet: one pats quarter notes, the other taps out eighths. But you can't count like a metronome. As slide ace Ry Cooder puts it: "Hooker has rhythmic tension in his feet; the guitar drives right down the middle. Tell me that isn't hip!"

Hooker, who picks exclusively with his thumb and index finger, uses an open *A* tuning (*EAEAC#E*, low to high) for most of his classic boogies. As you see in **Ex. 1**, the basic pulse happens on the upbeats. Begin by tapping out quarter-notes with one foot and backstroking strings three and four with your right index finger. Your

foot hits the downbeat, your finger sounds the accented upbeat. Play with a relaxed swing feel. (Think "one *and*," "two *and*," "three *and*," "four *and*": play "foot *stroke*," "foot *stroke*," "foot *stroke*.") Next, on the downbeat slap your left 2nd finger across strings three and four (try the 3rd fret) to produce a muted pitchless *doink*. This adds a percussive element and cuts the ringing open strings, further defining the rhythm. Finally, add the turnaround notes (beat four). Gradually work up to the indicated tempo.

Ex. 1

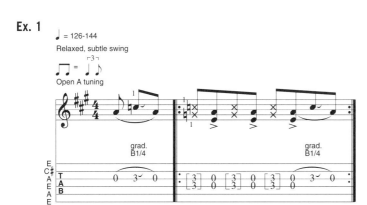

Ex. 2 kicks off with a classic Hooker pickup. Notice the variation in the last two beats of bar 2; throw this in occasionally to keep things interesting. In **Ex. 3**, Hooker drops the single-note figure down an octave, toughening up the groove. He also expands the boogie upbeat to a full *A* or *A7* chord. This time, mute the downbeats (beats two and three) with your right hand; drop your palm down on the strings nice and easy.

Ex. 2

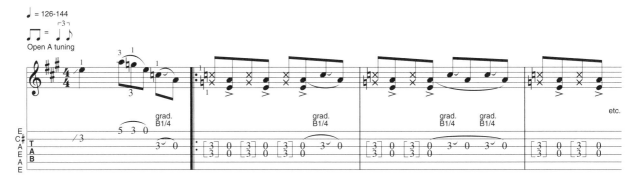

Ex. 3

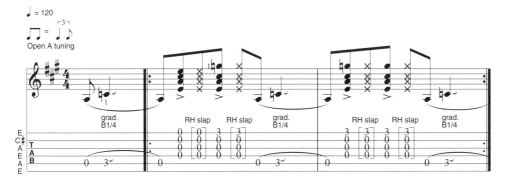

Hooker's boogie groove is usually deep and relentless. For contrast, however, he'll sometimes bring the proceedings to a grinding halt, using the *A7* triplets in **Ex. 4**. Pause on the last chord (bar 2, beat three). When the tension gets unbearable, release it by resuming the groove. **Ex. 5** shows another way John Lee temporarily breaks the groove. Ignore the pickup notes ("and" of beat 4) on the second repeat.

Ex. 4

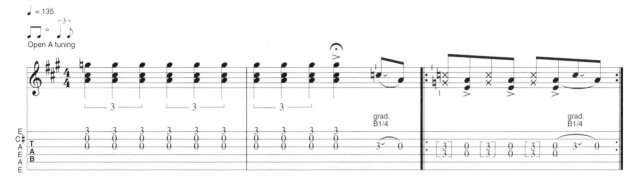

Ex. 5

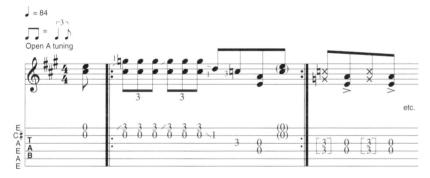

Working the bass, as in **Ex. 6a**, gives more of a rolling motion to the boogie—almost a half-time feel. **Ex. 6b** demonstrates another variation on this rolling theme. Bend the low *G♯* slightly as you play it.

Ex. 6a   **Ex. 6b**

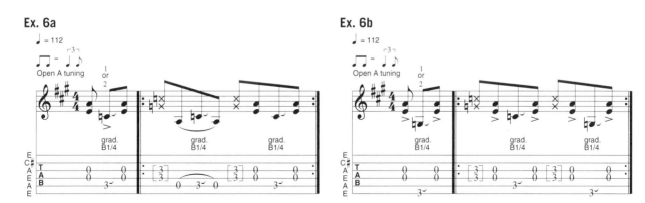

Sometimes John Lee plays the triplets in **Ex. 7**, treating them almost as a lead break. Practice this by itself, then try inserting it into a boogie. Not all boogies are in open *A* (**Ex. 8**). This familiar Hooker figure is in standard tuning. Mute with your outside right palm to choke the low *E*.

Ex. 7

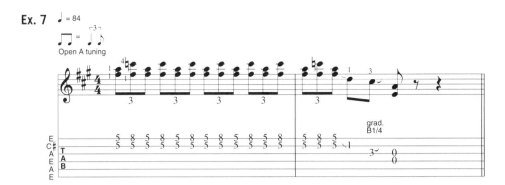

Ex. 8

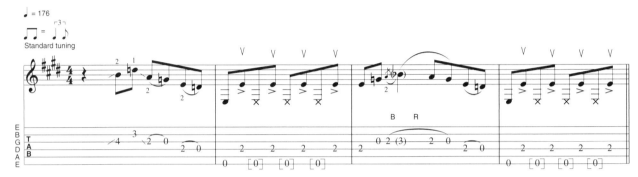

Ex. 9 illustrates how you can graft John Lee's cunning groove to a more hard-rockin' riff. We're back in open *A*; whether you use your thumb and 1st finger or a plectrum for this lick, follow the picking directions. Dial in plenty of gain on your amp for the full effect. **Ex. 10** carries the same rock-boogie approach into standard tuning. Every two bars you'll whomp all six open strings before hammering on a downbeat *E* chord. You have to perspire to make this sound right. On your mark, get set—boogie, chillen! ■

Ex. 9

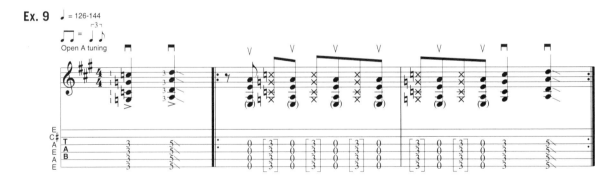

Ex. 10

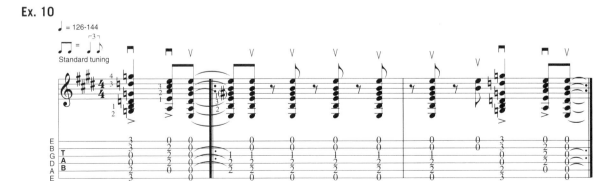

T-Bone Walker, late '40s

T-Bone Special

W T-Bone Walker's Electric Blues

BY ANDY ELLIS

When people start debating who played electric guitar first, just smile and let 'em squabble. What's more important is who saw the electric's potential in the late '30s and early '40s, approached it as a different instrument—not simply a louder archtop acoustic—and then used their amplified axes to change music forever. An electric guitar pioneer, T-Bone Walker grasped the potential for playing horn-like, single-note lines in blues and jump settings. He developed a bold new sound that influenced and inspired the greats who followed him. John Lee Hooker got his first electric guitar—an Epiphone archtop—from T-Bone. B.B. King said, "When I heard T-Bone Walker play the electric guitar, I just had to have one."

Walker was a consummate showman. Dancing and doing splits, he pushed electric guitar into the spotlight, helping make it the instrument of choice for cool cat wannabes. Buddy Guy admits to copping T-Bone's moves, and Jimi Hendrix borrowed many stage antics—such as playing behind his head—directly or indirectly from T-Bone, as did Stevie Ray Vaughan.

T-Bone's jazz-tinged jump blues sound has a number of characteristic elements. Grab the CD *T-Bone Blues*, which contains choice tracks from '55 to '57, and ponder the following as you listen:

- T-Bone featured the 9th scale degree prominently in his single-line solos. When you hear such players as Otis Rush, Buddy Guy, and Michael Bloomfield work a lick up to the 9, they're paying tribute to Mr. Walker.
- Influenced by horn players, T-Bone would spin long phrases across bar lines and chord changes, as heard on "T-Bone Blues." Even today, most blues guitarists typically play shorter licks. As Otis Rush said, "T-Bone had his shit very well placed, playing all those horn parts."
- A master of timing, T-Bone played subtle but intriguing games with the music's feel. Over a steady, slow shuffle such as "Mean Old World," he'd alternately move from a jazzy triplet swing to a straight eighth-note delivery. Or he might slip into a bluesy 12/8 feel while playing against a shuffling 4/4 dotted-eighth-note groove ("Blues for Marili").
- T-Bone frequently worked double-stops into tunes like "Shufflin' the Blues." Chuck Berry would later borrow these intervals, along with T-Bone's trademark third-to-second-string unison bends, to forge basic rock-and-roll guitar vocabulary.
- With the exception of those whole-step unison stretches, T-Bone relied primarily on half-step and quarter-step bends. Remember, slinky strings didn't exist in the '40s and '50s. It would take a younger crew to blaze the string-bending trail, as Albert King explained: "T-Bone had the sound I was looking for, but all those licks he was making I couldn't do. So I developed that string-squeezing sound."
- Unlike those he influenced so profoundly, Walker rarely used vibrato when sustaining or bending a note.
- T-Bone's archtop tone was dry, clean, woody, and—compared to that of hollowbody jazz players of the time—piercing.
- T-Bone picked his guitar with its face angled toward the sky. We can only speculate on how this affected his tone and phrasing, but it's reasonable to assume that by picking away from his body, rather than towards the floor the way most of us do, he'd lift the string a tad each time he picked it, increasing the snap of his attack.
- Walker favored sliding 9th chords ("Papa Ain't Salty," "T-Bone Blues," "Call It Stormy Monday") and popularized the use of chromatic dominant-7 and dominant-9 runways to the I7, IV7, and V7 changes. His was a high-toned, uptown blues sound.
- In the late '50s, T-Bone recorded with electric guitarists R.S. Rankin and Barney Kessel. Discerning listeners will hear each guitarist's distinct style. The quick-fretting Rankin liked to double-pick and favored a spanky, reverbed tone. Backing T-Bone, Kessel employed an aggressive attack, a rather dark timbre, and string sweeps. Kessel would sometimes focus on the low strings for his bop-inspired leads.

Break out an archtop, and let's investigate some characteristic T-Bone phrases.

Ex. 1 illustrates how T-Bone would work a lick across the high strings, peaking on the 9 (*A*, beat three). He also liked to bend into the ♭5 (*D♭*) from a half-step below—in this case, three times in two bars. Use downstrokes on bar 1's triplet and make the line swing.

Ex. 1

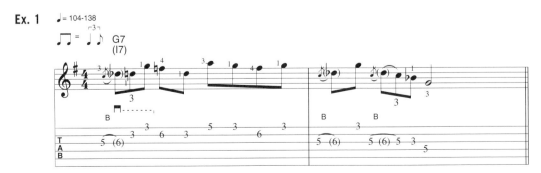

T-Bone would often emphasize the 9 by holding it longer than preceding notes and placing it on strong beats. Check out beats three (bar 1) and one (bar 2) in **Ex. 2**. There's the ♭5 again (bar 2), this time played as a slide rather than a bend.

Ex. 3 features both a bend into and a slide from the ♭5. Drop into the latter, bar two's fast ♭5-to-4 twitch, from the ♭7 (*F♮*) above. This T-Bone move is most cool. Finesse that last quarter-bend; make it subtle and sweet.

Ex. 2

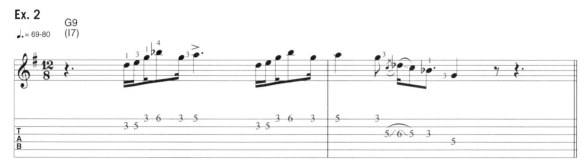

Ex. 3

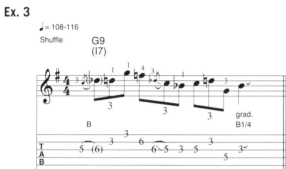

Train time! **Ex. 4** contains the world's hippest double-stops. Push beat three's quarter-bends a tad higher than the others. T-Bone surely had horns in mind when he picked this one. It's harmonically versatile: Do a whole chorus with it, playing over *C9, F9,* and *G9*—the I7, IV7, and V7 of *C*.

Ex. 4

Ex. 5 rolls the same bluesy double-stops into a strong IV7–I7 lick. Note the quarter-prebend in beat four. Chuck Berry made good use of this triplet move.

Here's an example of T-Bone's thematic lines (**Ex. 6**). See how he rolls a melodic motif across the bar lines? Observe the accents and listen for those 9's (*D*). There are recurring 6th tones (*A*) as well; they too play an important role in T-Bone's jivin' sound.

Ex. 5

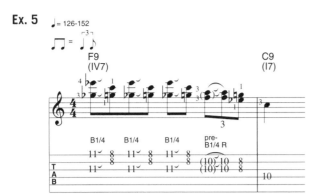

Ex. 6

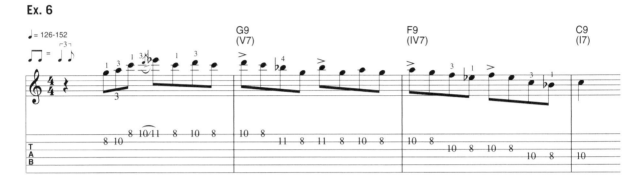

Ex. 7 moves a triplet motif across two bars, nailing the ♭5, ♭7, 9, 6, and ♭3 (*D♭, F♮, A, E, B♭*)—all colorful blues tones—and ending with a tangy quarter-bend.

Motif city: **Ex. 8**. Bar 1 opens with a greasy sliding lick that T-Bone immediately echoes an octave lower—rhythm, notes, and all. That tritone (*E–B♭*, bar 2, beat two) will spice up any blues line. You can play the entire two-bar phrase against *G9* (I7), the way T-Bone did, or divide bar 1 in half, granting *D9* (V7) and *C9* (IV7) two beats each before cruising to the I7 in bar 2.

Ex. 7

Ex. 8

A melodic gem, **Ex. 9** has a real sax vibe. Try a full, squawking tone and don't rush it.

Ex. 10 features half-step and quarter-step bends against a *D9–C9–G9* (V7–IV7–I7) cadence. Once you play the line, you'll hear the underlying theme: a whole-step, fifth- to third-fret dance across the top three strings.

Ex. 9

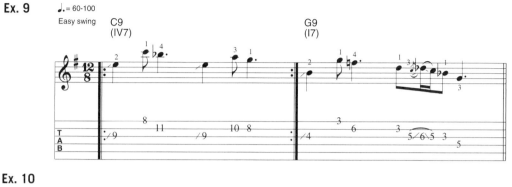

Ex. 10

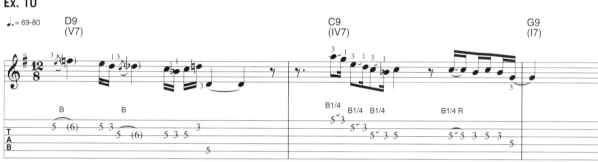

There are two neat string-skipping jumps in **Ex. 11**—from *D♭* to *G* and back (beats two and three). The half-step bends that follow are quick, so stay limber.

Like the previous line, **Ex. 12** has a double-time feel. The hip ingredients are all here: a repeated melodic and rhythmic motif, cool blues notes (especially the ♭5), a cresting 9, and even a minor/major hammer-on (*B♭–B♮*).

Ex. 11

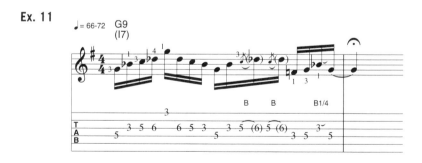

Ex. 12

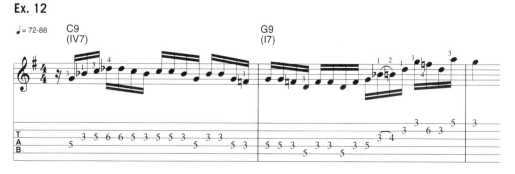

No T-Bone lesson would be complete without some dominant-9th chord voicings (**Ex. 13**). As you try the three forms, dig the close voicing, particularly between *C9* and *F9* (I7 and IV7). These chords share a pair of common tones; the other two notes simply swap fret position. At a variety of swinging tempos, play a 12-bar I7–IV7–V7 progression using these voicings and T-Bone's two-bar rhythm pattern.

Ex. 13

In "Stormy Monday," T-Bone pushes dominant-7th chords around in a most compelling way. **Ex. 14** is a favored turnaround. You can easily adapt it to any 12-bar blues. Go on—amaze your friends.

Ex. 14

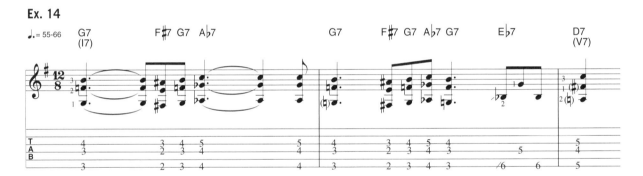

Next time you're out jamming or gigging, pay homage to the smooth and swinging T-Bone with a solo cooked up his way: Establish a motif and repeat it across the fretboard, ascend to the 9, work the ♭5, spin the phrase across two or more bar lines, and season the works with some tasty half- and quarter-step bends. Go, daddy-o!   ■

Albert Collins, 1991

© Clayton Call

Bone-Chilling Blues

A Lesson with the Mighty Albert Collins

BY ANDY ELLIS

The man had one helluva right hand. From five feet away, Albert Collins made his beat-up, unamplified Telecaster sound as loud as a Gibson 335 or even an old Kay archtop. Snapping and popping the strings, Collins poured himself into every note, even though his audience consisted of merely two *Guitar Player* staffers and his manager. Albert's sly grin made it abundantly clear that even after all those years, he still loved to play.

Collins's style is unique: His tone, sometimes cutting and reverb-drenched, sometimes hot and squawking, never fails to command complete attention. His stuttering, chicken-pickin' right-hand attack has as much to do with country as blues (no flatpick, folks, just a callused thumb and index finger). Then there's the business of the open tuning and capo.

Albert tuned to an open *Fm* chord (**Ex. 1**), which is how we've notated the following licks. Refer to the note placement chart (**Fig. 1**) to orient yourself on this fretboard while working out the examples. You can, of course, ignore the tab and play the licks in standard tuning, but it's worth the dues to retune and play them authentically. You'll get a deeper insight into the Iceman's way.

Ex. 1 Open Fm tuning

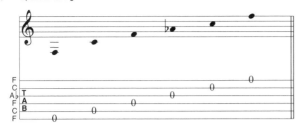

Fig. 1

Strings	6	5	4	3	2	1
open Fm	F	C	F	A♭	C	F
1st						
2nd	G	D	G	B♭	D	G
3rd				B		
4th				C	E	
5th	B♭	F	B♭	D♭	F	B♭
6th	B	G♭		D		
7th	C	G	C	E♭	G	C
8th	D♭	A♭	D♭	E	A♭	D♭
9th	D		D	F	A	
10th	E♭	B♭	E♭	G♭	B♭	E♭
11th			E			E
12th			F		C	F

Asked to illustrate how a classic blues lick lies on the fretboard in his open tuning, Albert clapped a capo on the 5th fret (producing an open B♭m chord) and served up **Ex. 2**. Notice how the open strings—courtesy of the capo—add an unexpected resonance to the line. Right away, you know you've taken leave of the B.B. King/Albert King school. For an approved funky feel, upstroke all the notes on the top three strings with your right index finger; snap strings four and five with your thumb. The funky minor/major hammers (bar 2, beat one) are a Collins trademark. **Ex. 3** features this minor/major interplay twice. Let the open strings ring (we're still capoed at the 5th fret) in beats three and four. Play with a hard swing feel and really flog the accented notes.

Ex. 2

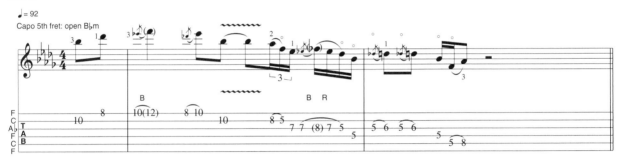

Ex. 3

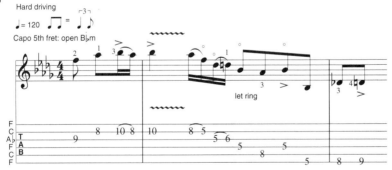

Albert singled out jazz organists as a major source of inspiration. As evidence, he offered **Ex. 4**. It's easy to imagine Brother Jack McDuff laying this one down at the Hammond. Emulate organ-key click by vigorously snapping the accents, and throw in some chicken-cluck by half-fretting bar 1's G♮s. How about those slinky double-stops in bar 2? Too cool. Try index upstrokes on all but the fifth string.

Ex. 4 Barroom swing
♩ = 108
Capo 5th fret: open B♭m

Ex. 5 contains more intriguing parallel harmony. Collins likened this to a big-band horn sound; he used such passages to sweeten his piercing single-note lines. When you pull off into the last chord, keep the open strings ringing against the G♮; the result is an ear-tweaking Gm7♭5. If you're into pretty chordwork, dig Albert's turnaround in **Ex. 6**: B♭m7–Gdim–G♭–B♭6. The passage starts minor and ends major, resembling the picardy third of baroque music. Use this as an ending to a minor blues tune and turn some heads.

Ex. 5 Barroom swing
♩ = 108
Capo 5th fret: open B♭m

Ex. 6
♩. = 69
Capo 5th fret: open B♭m

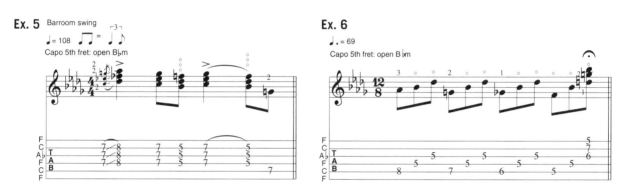

To get a feel for how Collins played over chord changes, give **Ex. 7** a whirl. The last beat of bar 1 boasts a foxy pull-and-slide maneuver. Such subtleties become rather meaningful when delivered through a Fender Quad Reverb on 10—Albert's typical stun setting. Once again, the open strings in bars 2 and 3 give the sound a distinctive, ringing quality. By twice emphasizing F♮ in bar 2, Collins outlined a dominant-9 sound against the IV7 chord. Go easy on bar 4's pull-off; you want to ghost that open third string. Finally, a subtle point: In bar 3, Collins elected to spank D♭ on the fourth string instead of going for the more obvious open third. The latter choice would leave two open strings ringing out a minor third at the end of the lick; his way sounds tougher. Try 'em both.

Ex. 7
♩ = 92-100
Capo 5th fret: open B♭m

F7 (V7)   E♭7 (IV7)   B♭m7 (Im7)

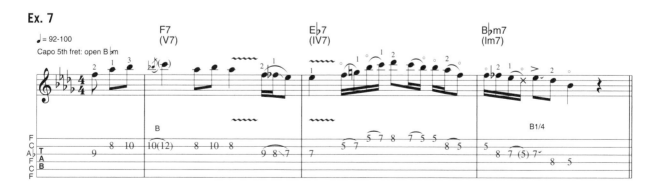

Octaves play a role in Albert's stinging sound. In his open minor tuning, they occur on parallel frets, paired on strings one and four, two and five, and—here's where the pattern changes—four and six. In **Ex. 8**, Collins kicks things off with a cool half-step slide. Squeeze the octaves with thumb and index. This time the ubiquitous minor- to major-third hammer occurs on the fourth string instead of the third. Make the last double-stop really staccato; after picking it, quickly mute the strings with your fretting fingers.

Ex. 8

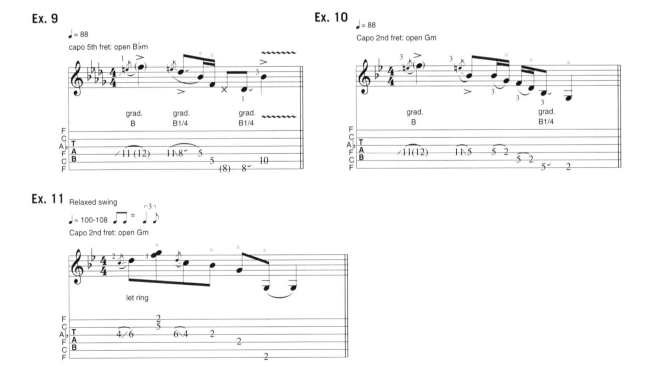

Albert's deep bag of tricks also included intriguing fourth-string swoops, such as in **Ex. 9**. The trick is to yank the string as hard as you can with your right thumb while sliding and bending. (It's okay to grimace during this procedure; the lick will sound more credible if you do.) Half-fret beat three for that chicken-pickin' thang. By fretting the last B♭ rather than picking the open fourth string, you can add vibrato to the note. **Ex. 10** uses a similar swooping technique against an open *Gm* chord, capoed at the second fret. Since you get more runway on this guy, you can get even more aggressive with the gliss. Have mercy! Albert favored open *Gm* for his more swampy styles; the lower notes give his sound girth. **Ex. 11**, he pointed out, is a Lightnin' Hopkins classic. It lays out nicely in this tuning, don't you think?

Ex. 9

Ex. 10

Ex. 11

Unless you saw Collins onstage with John Lee Hooker, you likely wouldn't have heard the Iceman's awesome take on "Boogie Chillun." Too bad: Albert surely had the feel, and his tuning suits the boogie to a "T" (**Ex. 12**). For that certified lowdown sound, thumb the sixth string and upstroke the rest with your index. After plucking the double-stops, quickly slap-mute the open strings with your left hand. Pop-pop, click-clack. When you get the train thing going, you're doing it right.

Ex. 12

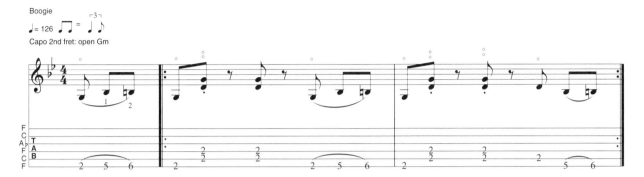

After chugging along in boogie mode for a while, Albert would come to a crashing halt in the spirit of John Lee and play **Ex. 13** at roughly half speed. Once the dissonance of beat three's diminished chord settles in, he would resume the boogie at full tempo. Regarding the chordal stuff: No fancy classical right-hand technique allowed. Just muster as much muscle as you can from one digit and lay on those nasty upstrokes.

Ex. 13

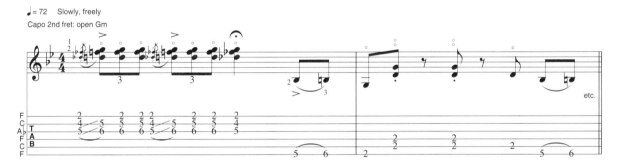

Ex. 14 is another cool boogie break. You can drop this one into Ex. 12's groove without slowing the tempo. Loop it, oh, three times before resuming the how-how-*how* stuff.

Ex. 14

Final Pointers

Albert usually strung his Tele with a set of .010s. Since he tuned higher than normal—that fifth string is taut, y'all—and capos as well, you know he played with a mighty tight setup. This helps explain his penetrating tone and gives new meaning to "high strung" guitar.

Collins generated all his chicken pickin' with left-hand half-fretting and ghosting. He kept his Tele's bridge cover on, you see, so right-hand palm muting is out of the question. "That's why I never play a Strat," confided Albert. "I rest my hand on the cover over the strings."

Perhaps the most important lesson we can glean from Albert is not related to tunings, capos, screaming Quad Reverbs, or string gauges. It's about attitude: When Collins played, he delivered every note with utter conviction. This take-no-prisoners approach is something we can all take to heart. ■

Peter Green

Rattlesnake Shake

Exploring Peter Green's Supernatural Blues

BY ANDY ELLIS

It's the little things—the timbral shadings, radical dynamics, and spot-on intonation—that make Peter Green's guitar playing so powerful and exciting. "Peter had a deftness, a touch, and a more melodic style," asserts Mike Vernon, who produced John Mayall's Bluesbreakers and all the early Fleetwood Mac albums—giving him the unique perspective of overseeing both Eric Clapton and Green in the studio. "He was the very best blues guitarist England ever produced."

In this lesson, we'll focus on details that characterize Green's lead lines. The goal is not to emulate Green, but to absorb some of his note choices and phrasing concepts. Once they've sunk in, you can integrate these ideas nicely with the blues techniques you already know.

This lesson's examples are all drawn from songs found in the six-CD set *Fleetwood Mac: The Horizon Years, 1967–1969*. In addition to offering remixed and remastered versions of familiar Mac albums, this collection includes many alternate, previously

unreleased versions of the band's classics—as well as a plethora of false starts, experiments, and studio banter. There's a wealth of Green licks to tackle, so grab a guitar, dial in a fat, relatively clean amp tone, and let's get rolling.

In his solos and fills, Green loves to incorporate two notes that lurk just outside the blues box. Taking a cue from B.B. King, Green jazzifies his lines by featuring the 2 and 6—tones not included in the blues scale per se.

Some background: The blues-scale formula is 1–♭3–4–♭5–♮5–♭7. [See "Tale of the Scale," page 6, for more]. Adding the 2 and the 6 expands the note palette by 30 percent. With this simple enhancement, our formula now reads 1– 2–♭3–4–♭5–♮5–6–♭7. You can think of this as a "swing" blues scale—a handy term that's bound to offend music-theory zealots. Excellent!

Now let's see where these tones lie and hear what they sound like. **Ex. 1** is drawn from a previously unreleased take of "Watch Out." The lads recorded this fast shuffle at a brisk quarter-note = 192. However, the line also works at slower tempos, so for starters, shoot for around 116 BPM.

We're in the key of B♭. See the accents on D♭, G, C, and B♭? Two of these notes—B♭ and D♭—are the 1 and ♭3 of the B♭ blues scale. But G and C are the 6 and 2—the "green" tones. Check it out: G, the 6, lies a minor 3rd below B♭, the 1, while C, the 2, occurs a whole-step above B♭. (To fully appreciate this phrase—in fact, all those in this lesson—be sure to listen to it with chordal accompaniment. Use a looper, recorder, or jamming partner to establish the harmony and backbeat.)

Ex. 1

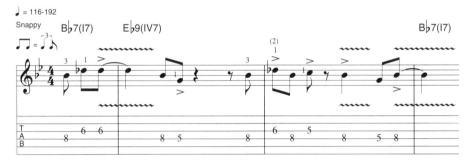

Another way to view these tones is in the context of the chord of the moment. Why does this lick peg E♭9, the IV7 chord? (Psst—dominant 9 chords function as dominant 7s, so E♭9 is simply a more elaborate version of E♭7.) When you accent G, you're emphasizing the 3 of E♭9 (1–3–5–♭7–9). In bar 3, the accents outline a ♭7-6-5 move against E♭9. Here, we have two chord tones linked by the 6.

Keep these two points in mind:

• There are always several ways to analyze a musical phrase.

• What matters most is making a line sound good. Analysis is simply a tool that helps you reconstruct a phrase in other keys or musical settings.

As you play Ex. 1, try to visualize the B♭ blues box. Do you see how the 6 (G) lies one fret below the ♭7 (A♭), and how the 2 (C) lies one fret below the ♭3 (D♭)? You can access these new notes by simply moving your 1st finger one fret back from the box position—easy.

For a neat variation of this lick, skip the three pickup notes. Instead of anticipating the downbeat, start right on beat one, bar 1. Ahh—but don't lose D♭'s vibrato.

Excerpted from another version of "Watch Out" (this one a medium shuffle in the key of A), **Ex. 2** illustrates another use of the 6 and 2. Here, Green moves to a higher register and encircles the root with these jazzy tones. This 16th-note embellishment (a favorite move of B.B. King and Michael Bloomfield) occurs on beat four. Keep the hammer and pull smooth and experiment with the fingering for the 6 (F♯). Clapton and other Brits smack the 2nd finger down on the second string. Another option is to use your 3rd finger.

Beat two's 3rd-finger bend requires backup—use your 1st and 2nd digits to add extra muscle. Green favored a fast, narrow vibrato, so where wiggle is indicated, think violin.

The next three examples (also from "Watch Out") all feature triplets. This three-notes-in-the-space-of-two rhythm plays a crucial role in Green's blues.

Ex. 2

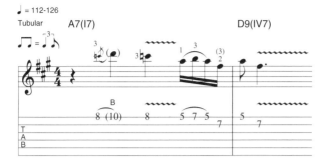

Played over an *A7–E9* change, **Ex. 3** features both quarter-note and eighth-note triplets. If you have difficulty counting the rhythm, tap it out on your guitar while a metronome or drum machine marks quarter-notes. Do this one hand at a time, then use both together.

Some technical tips: The trick is to hold that opening bend against the following two notes. This oblique bend gets tricky when you pick the high *F♯* over the sustaining, bent *C♯*. (In an oblique bend, you stretch one string while holding another still.) To make the maneuver easier, back your 2nd-finger bend with the 1st, and keep your 3rd finger planted on *E* when reaching for *F♯* with your 4th. This rigorous yet versatile move is also used in hot-rod country.

When you restate the oblique bend in beat three, play it staccato. This gives you time to reposition your fretting hand for beat four's pull-off.

Ex. 3

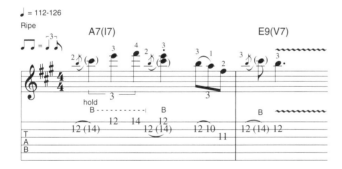

Ex. 4 also uses eighth-note and quarter-note triplets. This *E9–D9–A7* phrase contains a variation of the 1–2–1–6 encircling lick we first saw in **Ex. 2**. Play the same notes on the same beat, but this time in the tenth position as opposed to the fifth. To keep up with Green, you must master both versions in all keys.

Ex. 4

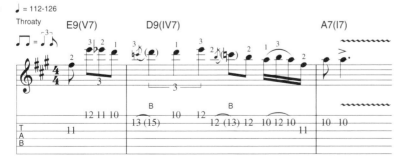

In "Watch Out" Green plays **Ex. 5** over *A7*, but the line also makes a nifty bridge from *D9* to *A7*. Here's why: It outlines a *D9* arpeggio in bar 1, and then anticipates *A7*'s root. The sly rests in beats two and three make Ex. 5 tricky. Try stroking muted strings during the rests: chuck-doo-dah, doo-dah-chuck. This approach lets you physically play three eighth-notes per triplet, even though two of the nine notes are technically silent. Once you've got the groove, simply drop the muted chucks. Don't overlook the accent and quarter-bend in beat four. Remember, it's all about details.

In Fleetwood Mac, Green bent notes with uncanny precision. **Ex. 6** comes from "Rollin' Man," a rumba blues. This phrase follows *D9* (the IV7) back to *A7* (the I7). The three bends in bar 2 are of particular interest: Notice how Green begins the series by stretching *B* a half-step to *C*, and ends it by stretching *B* to *C#*—*A7*'s 3. If you're feeling adventurous, try placing the middle bend right between these two notes. The difference is subtle, but the resulting microtonal note makes the ascent to *C#* even more dramatic. Keep your attacks crisp, sustain the bends for their full value, and play this lick with a full, cutting tone.

Ex. 5

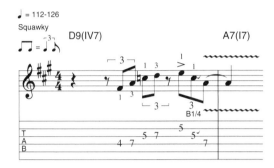

Ex. 6

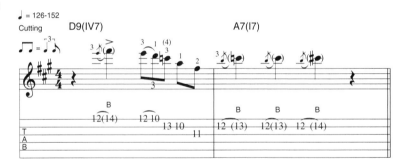

The Horizon Years contains multiple versions of "Need Your Love So Bad," a slow 12/8 blues ballad by Little Willie John. In over 44 minutes of experimentation—with and without string arrangements—Green plays dozens of juicy blues licks in the key of *A*. Let's explore a handful that revolve around *A* on the second string, 10th fret.

We'll begin with a trio of two-beat licks. **Ex. 7a** leads into *A7*, the I7. While Green uses variations of this classic B.B. King move to start off "Need Your Love So Bad," the figure also works to set up a solo. Crisply articulate the three pickup notes, and keep the whole-step bends smooth and even.

Another B.B.-inspired move, **Ex. 7b** leads nicely from *A7* to *D9*, the IV7 chord. For maximum contrast, give the opening bend its full value and then play the next two notes staccato. Accent the final *A*, and use "hummingbird" wrist vibrato to make it sing. [For a detailed description of this technique, see the "Two Kings" lesson, page 69.]

Another *A7*–*D9* transitional lick, **Ex. 7c** also benefits from wrist vibrato—but don't add it until you cross the bar line and enter *D9* territory. Once again, we have the 6 (*F#*) and 2 (*B*) encircling the root, *A*.

Ex. 7a

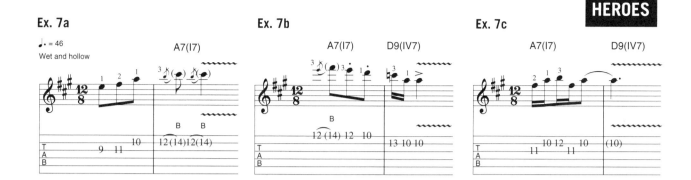

Ex. 7b

Ex. 7c

In **Ex. 8a**, which leads from *D9* back to *A7*, Green again follows a fat whole-step bend with two staccato notes (beat one). Beat two's pre-bend and release are key elements in London blues. It takes practice to silently stretch a string (in this case, moving *B* one half-step up to *C*) and have the target note be in tune when you finally attack it. To acquire this skill, alternately pick a fretted *C* (to imprint your sonic destination) and then, without picking *B*, push it toward you until you think you've bent a half-step. Now pick the bent note and compare it to the fretted *C*. Close? Repeat this drill—for days—until you can hit the target every time you try. The pre-bend physics change subtly as you move up and down the neck or when you switch to the first or third string, so practice the move all over the fretboard. Remember to work on whole-step pre-bends, too.

Ex. 8b introduces a new bending technique. In this phrase Green first bends a whole-step on the second string and then quickly shifts his hand down one fret to bend a half-step with the same finger. It helps if you stiffen your 1st, 2nd, and 3rd fingers and move them as a block from the higher to the lower position. Use your wrist and forearm—not finger muscles—to power these bends.

Ex. 8a

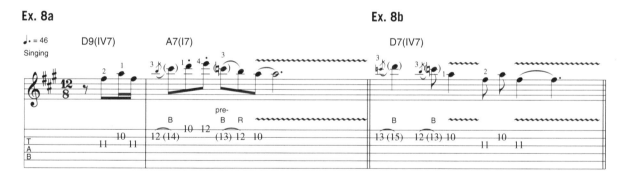

Ex. 8b

Yup, we're still drawing from "Need Your Love So Bad." **Ex. 9** begins with some cool double-stop action as Green moves from a major second to a fourth. The last pickup notes (beat four) contain a signature move: slide from ♭3 to 2, and then hit the root. Though few other blues players use this scalewise descent, you'll find it in many of Green's figures.

In bar 2, hear how Green outlines *A7* using the 3 (*C♯*) and 5 (*E*), and anticipates *E7* with an uptown *Eaug* arpeggio (*C♮–G♯–E*).

Ex. 9

Ex. 10 blends rhythmic sophistication and intriguing interval jumps. First, Green arpeggiates a root-position *D* triad against *Bm7*. This works because *Bm7* (*B–D–F♯–A*) contains a *D* triad (*D–F♯–A*). The descending jump from beat three's bent *C♯* to beat four's *E* is challenging—you have to silently release the whole-step bend while simultaneously dropping one string lower to play *E*. As you begin the transition, you may find it helpful to mute *C♯* with the side of your picking-hand thumb. There are a lot of notes, but the tempo is slow enough to let you finesse each one.

Ex. 10

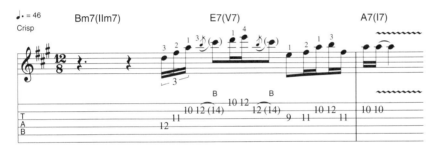

The swinging **Ex. 11** comes from a previously unissued take of "Stop Messin' Round." As you morph the tangy *D* quarter-bend into the *E♭* bend, be sure to give both notes a distinct attack. The five-note figure that carries you across the bar line is a rootless *F7* arpeggio. Memorize this gem—it makes a great gateway into the IV7 from either the V7 or the I7 and sounds great in all keys and registers. Because the first four notes occur on different strings, this arpeggio offers lots of "air" and timbral variety.

You have to be nimble to nail the double-stop pull and hammer (bar 2, beat three), so lighten your touch. The quarter-bend (beat four) adds soul to the Chuck Berry–like moves and hints at the hammered tritone (*B♭–E*) that kicks off bar 3.

Ex. 11

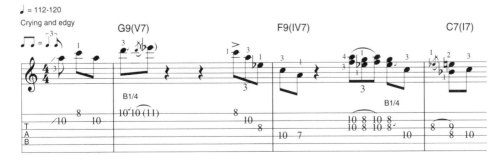

"If You Be My Baby" offers a cool lesson in subtle string stretching. First try **Ex. 12a**—this fits *D9*, the I7, like a glove. Not only does Green work his beloved 6, twice he bends the 2 a whole-step to tag *D9*'s 3 (*F#*). Now play **Ex. 12b**. This time we're heading into *G9*, the IV7. Changing only one note, Green bends a half-step, rather than the previous whole-step. The resulting *F♮* is *G9*'s ♭7.

Ex. 12a ♩ = 76-84
Snarky

Ex. 12b

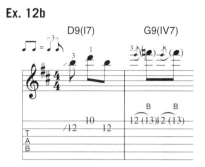

To recap: The whole-step bend hits the I7's 3, while the half-step bend hits the IV7's ♭7. This is a potent move—one worth learning in other positions. For instance, **Ex. 13a** moves the basic I7 line down an octave for a more sultry sound. Pick close to the bridge for extra twang. Next, using essentially the same fretting-hand grip, play **Ex. 13b**. Ahh—hear how this screams out the IV7 change? But again, only one note changes.

Ex. 13a ♩ = 76-89
Twangy

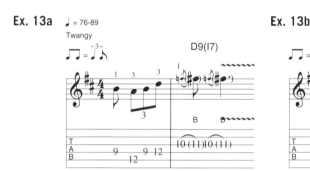

Ex. 13b

Let's take the concept a step further with a pair of swing-approved tritone slides. (An interval composed of three whole-steps, a tritone forms the heart of a dominant chord—its 3 and ♭7; for instance, *F#* and *C* in a *D7* chord) As in the previous four examples, we're still in the key of *D*. **Ex. 14a** provides a greasy pathway into *D9*—the I7. Again, using the same fretting grip, try **Ex. 14b**. Now we're setting up *G9*, the IV7. Cool, huh? In each example, give the tritone some soulful vibrato for a hornlike sound.

Ex. 14a ♩ = 76-89
Sassy

Ex. 14b

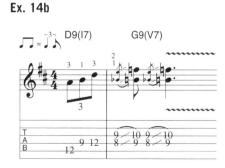

Be sure to audition Examples 12, 13, and 14 in all positions and keys. The payoff merits the effort, and your friends will wonder how you got so jazzy overnight.

No Peter Green lesson would be complete without some minor blues, so here's a lick inspired by "Fleetwood Mac"—an instrumental Green recorded with drummer Mick Fleetwood and bassist John McVie when all three were still members of John Mayall's Bluesbreakers. The tune is in the key of A♭ minor—presumably to accommodate the harp. For simplicity, let's transpose the lick to G minor.

A two-bar phrase, **Ex. 15** provides a moody transition from *Cm* to *Gm*, the IVm and Im. Play as legato as possible until you reach the accented double-stop. Green played this with his tone pot rolled back, so the original line sounds dark, woolly, and dry. The phrase also sounds groovy played bright and wet, so try it both ways. Bar 2 begins with the scalewise ♭3-2-1 descent we saw in Ex. 9. In this instance, however, we extend the move by one note to reach the ♭7 before bouncing back to the root.

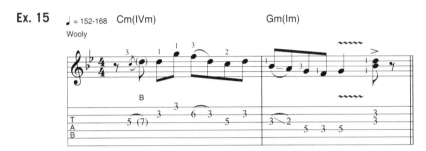

"Lazy Poker Blues" is a rollicking shuffle, giving Green plenty of opportunity to stretch out with hollow-toned leads. **Ex. 16** captures a slick line he uses to move from *E9* (the I7) to *A9* (the IV7). In beats three and four, notice how Green's patented ♭3-2-1 descent leads down to the 6. Shake the last *C♯*—it's *A9*'s 3, and you want to draw attention to it.

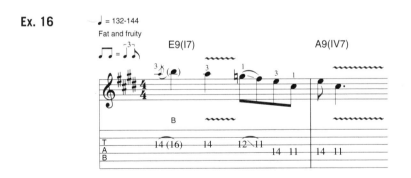

Ex. 17—also from "Lazy Poker Blues"—takes us from *A9* back to *E9*. The opening bends are really cool—first a whole-step from the 12th fret (with the 3rd finger), then a half-step from the 11th fret (using the 2nd finger). As always, back up the bending digit with any available buddies.

Ex. 17

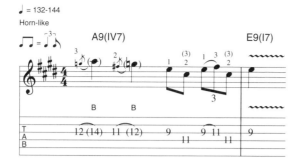

Green recorded many of his solos live with the band, so his vocal mic captures him humming, singing, and groaning along with his lines. Besides sounding cool, this offers an important lesson: If you want your leads to sound melodic, vocalize them while you're playing. It's a simple concept that most of us tend to overlook. You can change your playing immediately by simply refusing to finger something that you can't sing. While this technique isn't appropriate for certain flavors of jazz, shred metal, bluegrass, or hot-rod country, it certainly makes blues solos come alive.

Buddy Guy

Get Real

Buddy Guy, Hubert Sumlin, and Robben Ford on What It Takes to Play Genuine Blues

BY ADAM LEVY

As anyone who has taken a few guitar lessons knows, a student asking a teacher how to play blues guitar is usually shown the minor-pentatonic scale in a couple of positions and sent on his or her merry way. Is that really all there is to playing the blues?

Apparently not. Otherwise, every 12-year-old with a Fender Squier Strat would be a bona fide blues genius. (And, last we checked, that wasn't the case). Along similar lines, many of us have had the experience of ambling into a local drinking establishment to check out a live blues band, only to leave after a song or two because the guitarist didn't have the right stuff. The message is clear: There is more to blues than just I–IV–V progressions, pentatonic scales, and a couple of hackneyed Jimmy Reed riffs. So what do the real cats have that many of us don't? We wanted to know—so we asked them. Want to really play the blues? Take a seat, because Robben Ford, Buddy Guy, and Hubert Sumlin are about to give you some schooling in the art of the blues.

Robben Ford

Robben Ford describes his musical career as "a passionate musical journey that started with the blues." Ford's quest encompasses his work with blues shouter Jimmy Witherspoon to gigs with artists such as Joni Mitchell, Miles Davis, and Rickie Lee Jones, and all the way back to the blues. His first guitar hero was Michael Bloomfield. "In fact," Ford confesses, "there was a time when I sounded exactly like him. All I played were Mike Bloomfield licks."

Ford pegs the Paul Butterfield Blues Band's eponymous debut album as the Bloomfield recording that got him hooked on the blues. "All the music I had heard up to that point was the pop music of the day—bands such as the Beatles and the Stones," he says. "And, with all due respect, none of those guys were playing the hell out of the guitar like Bloomfield was. I got terribly excited and started focusing on playing electric blues guitar.

"By the time I was in high school and playing gigs, nearly all the music they played on the radio was R&B. I heard Otis Redding, Junior Walker & the All-Stars, Booker T. & the MG's, and Aretha Franklin. It was a good time to be learning because we were hearing all these soulful singers and bands, and that's the main ingredient of the blues—that soulful feeling."

The sounds of soul singers—Redding and Franklin in particular—influenced Ford's blues guitar phrasing. "The blues is vocal music," he says. "That's the truth. Good blues guitar playing has to come from the same place as singing does. You're using notes—not words—but you're saying the same things."

As Ford continued to develop, he began to study the music of jazz saxophonists such as John Coltrane and Wayne Shorter. "Listening to horn players and letting what they did come into my playing was really important in developing my own style. It fed me on a more harmonically and melodically sophisticated level."

But even through that period—which took place during Ford's early 20s—he continued to be drawn toward simpler forms of music. "That was a carryover from my blues roots. It was like, 'Let's not make this so difficult that we have to think too much and we can't actually enjoy ourselves.' I mean, I have the desire to be able to play a lot of great stuff really fast. But there wasn't enough heart in that kind of music to keep me going that way. I preferred to write simple tunes, get together with good musicians, and blow my brains out—as often as possible. So really, I learned by listening, listening, listening, and playing, playing, playing."

Buddy Guy

Buddy Guy's blues expertise came the hard way. He's a self-taught player with no formal training—except for a couple of lessons with a high school music teacher who, to Guy's disappointment, couldn't show him the things he really wanted to learn.

"I moved to Baton Rouge, Louisiana, to go to high school," he recalls. "And they had

B.B. King & John Lee Hooker on Being Yourself

To play great blues, you must first develop your musical personality. Each player's nuances of tone and phrasing become his or her calling card—as individual and identifiable as a fingerprint. This point was eloquently illustrated by B.B. King and John Lee Hooker in a Sept. '93 *Guitar Player* interview.

King: John has played so many different guitars through the years, and they all sound like John.

Hooker: I got my identity. I got my style. I wouldn't change for all the tea in China and all the money in the world. Who else you gonna sound like?

King: It's just like a piano that sits over in the corner. If John go and play it, he gonna sound like himself, 'cause that's the way he play. If I go play it, I'm gonna sound like myself, 'cause that's the way I play. That's just one of the things that we were blessed to be able to do—to be ourselves and do our own style.

Jonny Lang on "Absorption"

Jonny Lang says he got the blues in his blood by listening to his heroes—Albert Collins and B.B. King—and tracing their moves on his guitar. "I listened to all the best 'teachers' on CDs," he says, adding that he sometimes listened without a guitar in his hands, to absorb the music indirectly. "It's also important to find someone who can show you how to play some of your favorite guitarists' licks. After you've got a vocabulary of licks, you can start stringing them together your own way. Eventually, it becomes second nature. It's like learning to speak a foreign language: You learn a few words, put them together to make sentences, and pretty soon you do it without thinking about it.

"I also found that, after I listened to a particular guitarist or a style of music, some little part of what I was hearing came out when I played a show. It's how you perceive and absorb music that helps you develop your style—that's the way it happened for me."

a music teacher there, and I thought, 'My God, I've got what I've always wanted. I'm gonna let this guy teach me how to play the guitar.' I went in, and the teacher showed me some scales, and I said, 'I don't wanna play that; I wanna play like this'—I had a Muddy Waters record and a John Lee Hooker record at the time. He looked at me and said, 'I can't teach you that.' So I said, 'Well, then I can't take a music class!' I was so excited by the way Muddy played the slide, how B.B. King squeezed the strings, and how Lightnin' Hopkins and T-Bone Walker played their things. I said, 'If they don't teach this in school, I've got to find it myself.'

"Nowadays young people have advantages that I didn't have. It wasn't until 20 or 30 years ago that you even saw blues written in music notation—they claimed they couldn't write it. Now kids can watch videotapes of great blues players and pick up exactly what their fingers are doing. They can stop the tape and see what I didn't see when I was learning."

One tremendous benefit Guy had—after moving to Chicago in 1957—was seeing Chicago blues legends such as Muddy Waters, Wayne Bennett, Matt Murphy, and Earl Hooker when they were at the height of their powers. But no matter what a musician's cultural advantages—or disadvantages—might be, Guy maintains that anyone with enough heart can play the blues. "If you love the blues, you can play it. Every interview I've ever had, I get asked 'Can a white man play the blues?' I hate that question! It's a human being, man. If I had eight fingers on my left hand, then I would say, 'No, a white man probably can't play like me.' But these guys, man—the late Stevie Ray Vaughan, this young Jonny Lang, Eric Clapton, and Jeff Beck, to name a few—there's some things they do that I wish I had known.

"Look at athletes—boxers, football players, baseball players—they come in all sizes and all colors, and all those guys are great. Music is the same way. There's no advantage or disadvantage. If you want to learn this thing, man, and you love it the way I love it, you can do it."

Hubert Sumlin

Blues journeyman Hubert Sumlin has been playing guitar professionally for more than half a century. His first gig was with ace blues-harmonica player James Cotton when Sumlin was just 16 years old. A few years later, he took up residency in Howlin' Wolf's band—a gig that lasted until Wolf's passing in 1976. The fruits of their extraordinary musical partnership produced the hits "Killing Floor," "Smokestack Lightnin'," and "300 Pounds of Joy," among others.

Asked what it takes to become a real blues player, Sumlin offers this timeless advice: Study the recordings of the greats. His own first meeting with blues guitar mastery came via a record he found by accident.

Kenny Wayne Shepherd on Vibrato

With almost constant touring since the 1997 release of his second album, *Trouble Is...*, Kenny Wayne Shepherd has learned plenty about what it takes to play the blues for keeps.

"Once you get your basic skills down," he says, "you need to work on your vibrato. That's very important in the blues. There are different kinds of vibrato: pulling down and away from the neck, bending up into the neck, bending up and down—basically, you just have to hit a note and start working with it. It has taken me a few years to get my vibrato up to par, and I'm still working hard to perfect it."

Shepherd maintains that taking your blues playing to the next level requires getting out and gigging. "That's where you start being spontaneous and throwing your own stuff out there; where you go beyond merely playing the solos you've copied. And you can't just play—you've got to entertain. The players you admire should influence your performance as well as your playing. Hendrix has given me a lot of ideas to work from. I like the move where he squats down and throws the guitar between his legs. He's pretty much making love to the guitar. When Stevie Ray would do 'Third Stone from the Sun' live, he'd throw his guitar around like Hendrix, too."

"I found this old warped phonograph record in a garbage can," Sumlin recalls. "It was a Charley Patton record. I took it home and listened to it, and there was something about this guy—his singing, with all this mumbling and stuff going on, and his playing—it put something into me, man. I said 'This is what I'm gonna do.'"

Sumlin did his best to figure out what Patton was doing, and he started listening to other players, picking up whatever he could from wherever he could. "All this stuff, you sit down and listen to it, and it's just like going to school," he says.

Sumlin continued to gather ideas from a variety of sources, spinning the influences into his own distinctive style. "I've got jazz, I've got rock 'n' roll, I've got some of every record you ever want to name in your life. I'll take a note from you, put it with mine, and you'll think it's me—which it is, 'cause I make it me. I got my own sound, my own tone, and my own thing.

"You got to find yourself if you're gonna play this stuff. You know what these guys did—Muddy, Wolf, Stevie Ray, and all the rest. Think about them, fine, but be yourself. I got kids coming to me now, they want to know, 'How can I sound like you?' I say, 'Look here, you ain't me.' I had to find my own self in this business. You got to."

Not surprisingly, an ample measure of confidence is another essential ingredient in Sumlin's recipe for blues success. "You got to know that you can do it. There ain't no such thing as 'you can't do it.' You can. You can do anything you want to do—especially with a guitar."

The sermon is not over yet. Sumlin wants to make it clear that students of the blues must take the music seriously because it's not just about licks—it's a lifelong commitment: "I would advise anyone who's trying to learn this music to find what they want to do. Do you want to do this? Do you love this? You got to love it, you got to sleep it, you got to eat it—that's what it's all about, man." ■

Setting Up Your Axe for Serious Blues Action

Illustration by David Beck

BY DAN ERLEWINE

A guitar that's out of tune or hard to play is not "close enough for the blues." But blues guitar setups are a little easier than most because the buzzing and dead notes caused by light strings, fretboard radius, and other factors are less apparent when the strings are raised—and most blues players seem to prefer higher action.

Here are some points to consider when setting up a "blues" guitar—electric or acoustic—that will not only help you play better, but may also influence your next instrument purchase.

Scale length is worth considering when choosing any guitar. Understanding why it's important will help your blues playing—especially in terms of bends and left-hand reach.

Most electric and acoustic steel-string guitars use either a "short" 24¾-inch scale (Gibson), the "long" 25½-inch scale (Fender, Gibson, and others), or something in between (PRS compromises with its 25-inch scale). Martin's short and long scales are 24.9-inch and 25.4-inch. With its reduced string tension, the short scale is easier to bend on, responds more quickly to the touch, and lets small hands span greater distances. Short-scale guitars make the best fingerpicking instruments.

Because of its higher string tension, the long scale is louder and more powerful, has better individual note separation and definition, allows for heavier pick attack, and offers a brighter, tighter sound. But a long scale is also harder to bend on, and long reaches are more difficult. According to luthier Tim Shaw, "When you play a chord on a short-scale guitar, like most of the Gibsons used for blues, the strings blend well and sound like a family singing together. On the other hand, chords played on the long scale sound more like hired professional singers—clean and perfect, but without the blend. As for hand size, when I play the basic two-string blues shuffle rhythm in *F* [**Ex. 1**] on a long scale, my left-hand 4th finger barely reaches the 5th fret, but I can get it easily on a short scale."

Fretboard Radius

Fretboard radius determines how close you can set your strings to the frets while still being able to bend the first and second strings without "bottoming out"—an Albert King-ism for a dead note that is caused by the bent string running into the slope of the fretboard. Most vintage Fenders used a 7¼-inch radius, while Gibsons used a 12-inch measurement. The more-exaggerated Fender radius follows the hand's natural curve and facilitates barre chords, but the tight curve may cause "bottoming." Many current Fenders have a flatter radius, but the company's vintage replicas retain the 7¼-inch dimension. Gibson's 12-inch radius has always facilitated blues bending with no bottoming out, even with low action. Martin's flatter 16- to 20-inch radius has never presented bending problems.

Fret Height

Tall frets are much easier to bend on than low ones. Optimum fret height for a blues setup ranges between .035- and .055-inch. Frets lower than .030 begin to give poor results because they don't hold the string far enough from the fretboard to prevent your finger from slipping off when it grabs and pushes. Fretwire for blues (and most modern guitar playing) falls into two size ranges: "thin," which is .078 to .090 wide and .038 to .050 tall (Fender, Martin, Gretsch, and some older Gibsons); and "wide," which is .093 to 108 wide and .038 to .050 tall (Gibson and most others). While .055 to .060 extra-tall wire is available in either width and is great for bending, you may find it too tall for blues chord slides, like the famous "6th to 9th" we all use from time to time (**Ex. 2**).

Ex. 1

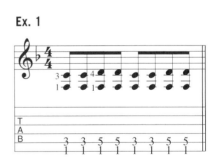

Ex. 2

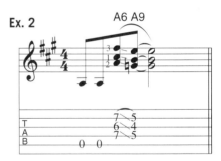

Nut slots always affect sound and playability. Normally, string slots are cut no deeper than one-half of a string's diameter, so that the strings don't become pinched or "muted." A blues setup, though, may require somewhat deeper slots on the treble strings, since a first-string bend can cause the *B* string to pop out, especially when bending 2nd-fret *F♯* up to *G* or *G♯*. In this case, the short section of string between the fretted note and the nut is extremely taut, and you'll pop the string if you tend to slip your finger under the open *B* string.

String Gauge

String gauge affects your style a lot, so experiment with all the gauges—from ultra-light to fairly heavy. But remember that each time you significantly change string gauge, you also change your setup. This will result in either spending some dollars at the local repair shop or learning to do the job yourself. Generally, the heavier the strings, the better the resistance to pick attack, so you can play things such as bass-string boogie/shuffle rhythms harder and with more drive.

Get used to a heavier string gauge gradually. For instance, don't bend a .012 first string without first toughening up. Otherwise, you risk getting "split nails," where the flesh of your finger pulls away from the nail. Splits are common and take about a week to go away. I've made it through many a night's playing by super-gluing the split, but I don't know if this is medically sound. Stevie Ray constantly glued his split nails.

Albert King may be the most-copied blues player in the world, so he had a good thing going. He tuned way below concert pitch—*CFCFAD,* low to high—which for years allowed him to use Black Diamond silver-wound heavy-gauge acoustic strings and still be able to bend. Albert later used this set: .009, .012, .024 (wound), .028, .038, and .050. If you're studying Albert's style, try his tuning and strings—he didn't seem to prefer a particular brand—and you'll be surprised. Stevie Ray Vaughan also tuned low, but only a half-step. His strings measured a hefty .013, .015, .019, .028, .038, and .058. Even tuned down a half-step, you need extremely strong hands to do what he did.

On an electric guitar, anything less than a .010–.046 set is a little light for me, but I admit to occasionally using a .009 high *E*. For years I preferred Gibson E-340 L Sonomatics (.011–.056) because Otis Rush used them in the early '70s. E-340 Ls came with a .019 wound third that sounded great; you could bend it, but it broke all the time. Substitute an unwound .020 for the *G*, and you'll have a good, fairly heavy set.

For the average acoustic player, light-gauge strings are best for blues, unless the guitar is very old and can't support them. Extra- and ultra-light strings won't strengthen your hands or draw out that "different" style of music inside you. Medium-gauge strings may be too heavy for the tops of many acoustics, so have your local repair shop check out your instrument before you take the plunge. Strong hands are a must for playing good blues on medium-gauge strings.

Action

Most electric guitars have adjustable bridges and necks, so setting action is relatively easy. As a precautionary measure, have a pro adjust your neck initially, and be sure to find out if the trussrod is working well. Necks are adjusted either perfectly straight or with "relief," a slight bow toward the strings' pull. Relief makes room for a vibrating string's elliptical pattern and helps avoid fret buzzing. You straighten a neck by tightening the trussrod and relieve it by loosening the rod. There are hundreds of possibilities between straight and relieved necks, high or low string settings, and different string gauges, which is why you should learn to adjust your own neck and bridge. You may never know what setup is best until you've tried them all, so here are some tips:

- You may like a neck that's adjusted as straight as you can get away with—find out by experimenting.
- You'll need a few simple tools and at least a whole day to experiment.
- The heavier the strings and higher the action, the straighter you can adjust the neck.
- Light strings close to the fretboard need more relief.
- Short scales tend to buzz more easily if the strings are too low, so they need more relief.
- Fret buzzes not heard through your amp are okay.
- Straight necks and low action may work if you play with a light touch and a loud amp setting. Don't expect to bend notes very far with this setup.
- Gibson action can be adjusted more easily than Fender action because the entire bridge raises and lowers on two thumbwheels, whereas most Fender bridges—Strats in particular—have an adjustable bridge saddle for each string.
- Electric or acoustics relief could measures anywhere from .003- to .015-inch in the 7th- to 9th-fret area.
- Raising an acoustic's action at the bridge may require reshaping the saddle, which

should probably be done by a pro. Sometimes you can simply shim or un-shim the saddle's height.

To set your own action, start with the neck straight and lower the strings at the bridge until they buzz badly. Next slowly raise the bridge or individual saddles until the buzzing barely stops, and see how the action feels; you'll probably have a medium-low action that buzzes with relatively firm pick attack.

Now give the neck a little relief and recheck the action. The buzzes should stop. The action will be higher, and you may end up liking this setup. If the buzzing doesn't stop, add relief until either it does go away or the up-bow is so ridiculous that it feels uncomfortable. If you have to start over by re-straightening the neck and re-lowering the strings, try raising the bridge until the buzzing stops. You might like this medium-high strings/straight neck setup.

Three Blues Setups

The measurements in **Fig. 1** were taken from a long-scale '56 Fender Strat, a short-scale '59 Gibson ES-345, and a 1944 short-scale Gibson J-45 acoustic—all guitars that were good examples of their type. In each case, the guitars were lying on their sides in the true playing position when I measured them. Using a steel scale and a set of feeler gauges, I recorded the distance between the *bottom* of the first and sixth strings and the *top* of the 1st and 12th frets.

On the action/playability scale, I rate these setups like this:

1. The Strat had a low to average "normal" action. It played well, and the strings were easy to bend.
2. The ES-345 had a very low setup. Since it was a brand-new fret job, I was able to get the neck perfectly straight without buzz.
3. The light-gauge strings on the J-45 provided enough tension so that the neck could be kept straight. It had low to medium action and played great.

Fig. 1			
Guitar	**Clearance**		**Relief**
	1st fret high *E*–low *E*	12th fret high *E*–low *E*	
Strat	.014–.034	.063–.094	.009
ES-345	.010–.024	.031–.047	none
J-45	.013–.022	.094–.109	none
All measurements in inches.			

Pickups

Electric blues is played with humbucking or single-coil pickups and combinations thereof. B.B., Albert, and Freddie King, early Eric Clapton, and the Allman Brothers all have a humbucking sound—a characteristic of Gibson ES-series semi-hollowbodies, SGs, and Les Pauls. For the single-coil sound, I think of Buddy Guy, Otis Rush, Magic Sam, and most of the current younger players like Robert Cray, Anson Funderburgh, Jimmie Vaughan, and the late Stevie Ray, all of whom use Fender Strats.

A Telecaster also offers an excellent single-coil blues sound, but it isn't used as often. Some of the greatest blues guitars are the Gibson archtop hollowbodies (used by T-Bone Walker, Chuck Berry, and many '50s rockers), including the ES-295, the ES-300, the ES-350, and the ES-5 Switchmaster. Many of these early guitars were powered by "soap-bar" single-coil pickups and have a sound all their own.

As a rule, Gibson guitars—even with single-coil pickups—have more sustain, a fatter, thicker overall sound, and more output than Fenders. Strats are more percussive sounding than Gibsons, but they have less sustain, unless you add distortion.

Setting Up for Slide

Setting up a guitar for slide or bottlenecking is fairly easy and non-invasive. Say, for example, you have an unused, Japanese-made Tele sitting in your closet. Here's how to optimize it for slide:

Step 1. Put on heavier strings. Gauges as high as .012–.054 are great for lower tunings—such as open D and open G—but if you want to be able to bottleneck and bend strings, go just one gauge higher than normal. If you decide to use much heavier strings, you may also have to widen your guitar's nut slots a bit to prevent the nut from cracking.

Step 2. Raise the bridge saddles until the action is high enough to keep the strings from bottoming out against the frets under slide pressure. (While you're at it, you may want to slightly flatten the string radius to better accommodate the slide.) It may also be necessary to loosen the trussrod a bit in order to introduce more relief (or back-bow) into the neck. But chances are that simply installing heavier strings will create the desired neck relief.

A "cheater" or Dobro nut (available from most music stores) can be slipped over the stock nut to raise the action up to ⅜-inch or higher, but it's only necessary to do this if the guitar is to be played lap style using a heavy steel bar.

Step 3. Once you dial in the action, the bridge pickup may need to be lowered a tad to prevent the strings from coming too close to the polepieces when you bear down with the slide—especially in the high registers. (If your pickups have adjustable polepieces, now is the time to tweak them to follow the string radius.)

Acoustic tricks. Converting a flat-top into a slide guitar involves the same steps. But in order to raise the bridge height on an acoustic, you'll need to install a shim (such as a slice of wood veneer or business card) under the saddle. Another alternative is to install a new, taller saddle with a flatter radius.

If your guitar is equipped with an under-saddle piezo pickup, remove it (after taking out the saddle) so that the shim can be placed under the pickup. This keeps the acoustic-electric sound intact by maintaining direct contact between the pickup and the saddle. Use caution when removing under-saddle pickups, as they can be damaged when pulled sideways (or at an angle). Always pull the pickup straight out, and slip your free hand inside the guitar body to push the cable up through the bridge.

—Gary Brawer

Flat-Tops

Acoustic guitars draw a different style of blues performance from you, which is why they are so refreshing to play. To me, ideal guitars for playing acoustic blues have a shorter scale length, which leaves out most of the larger dreadnoughts. Of course, you can play blues on a large guitar—Brownie McGee played a Martin D-18—you just have to work harder.

My favorite acoustic blues guitars are the early Gibson J-45, J-35, and the smaller L-0 or L-00 series, and all Martin 0-series models in either the 18 or 28 style (Big Bill Broonzy played a 000-28).

Vintage blues guitar expert Dave Hussong of Fretware Guitars says: "Some customers put the cart before the horse when they shop for a blues guitar; if B.B. used an ES-345 with an Ampeg Gemini II amp, they've got to have the same equipment. But the great players can produce their sound on just about any guitar. Hound Dog Taylor did fine with an Airline. The style overrides the instrument. You get the best blues setup only after your style has developed. If you're just getting into blues, don't rush out and buy a guitar until you've played for a year or so. Use what you have, unless you're worried about all the great vintage blues guitars getting bought up.

"Fretwire size has never made much difference to me, but rosewood boards and big frets generally produce a big tone, and maple necks with smaller frets give you the brighter tone. I don't like low action and still subscribe to the Texas school of players like T-Bone Walker, Lowell Fulson, and others, which means that I use as heavy a string as I can handle. Right now I'm playing an .011–.050 set.

"My two favorite blues guitars are a 1960 Shoreline Gold Fender Strat, which is on loan to me from Anson Funderburgh, and a 1962 Gibson ES-355 with the wide 1¹¹⁄₁₆" neck. If you've been playing a Strat and then pick up the Gibson, it's like a ball player laying down his heavy practice bat as he steps up to the plate. You've got to fight the Strat more, whereas the Gibson is easier to play. But a Strat has a certain tone all its own. When you're out there playing, you're more committed on a Strat—which also means your mistakes will be more obvious." ∎

Listen Up! A Blues Guitar Discography

"If you begin studying blues with Robert Johnson, you are really starting in the middle," says latter-day bluesman Paul Rishell in Art Tipaldi's *Children of the Blues: 49 Musicians Shaping a New Blues Tradition* [Backbeat]. With that in mind, in this discography we've listed recordings by a number of seminal, essential blues guitarists in addition to work by the artists our lessons cite. We've also included some of the great guitarists who are currently keeping the blues flame alive. The recordings are grouped by regional and chronological categories, but keep in mind many of these artists spanned schools, styles, and decades. These recordings merely sample the deep and wide world of blues guitar. To dig further, check Backbeat's *All Music Guide to Blues* and the blues links at allmusic.com.

DELTA

Skip James (1902–1969)
The Complete Early Recordings, Yazoo

John Lee Hooker (1920–2001)
The Very Best of John Lee Hooker, Rhino

Robert Johnson (1911–1938)
The Complete Recordings Columbia

Charley Patton (1887–1934)
Founder of the Delta Blues Yazoo

PIEDMONT

Blind Blake (c.1890–1933)
The Best of Blind Blake Yazoo

Lonnie Johnson (1899–1970)
Steppin' on the Blues Columbia

Blind Willie McTell (1901–1959)
The Definitive Blind Will McTell, Sony Legacy

MEMPHIS

Albert King (1923–1992)
Born Under a Bad Sign Rhino

B.B. King
Live at the Regal, MCA
Completely Well, MCA

Memphis Minnie (1897–1973)
Hoodoo Lady (1933–1937) Sony

TEXAS

Albert Collins (1932–1993)
Deluxe Edition, Alligator

Lightnin' Hopkins (1912–1982)
Blues Masters: The Very Best of Lightnin' Hopkins, Rhino

Blind Lemon Jefferson (1897–1929)
King of the Country Blues Yazoo

T-Bone Walker (1910–1975)
T-Bone Blues, Atlantic Jazz

Freddie King (1934–1976)
Ultimate Collection, Hip-O

Stevie Ray Vaughan (1954–1990)
In Step, Epic/Legacy

Greatest Hits, Epic

Johnny Winter
Johnny Winter, Columbia

Deluxe Edition, Alligator

CHICAGO

Buddy Guy
The Very Best of Buddy Guy Rhino

Elmore James (1918–1963)
The Sky Is Crying: The History of Elmore James Rhino

Magic Sam (1937–1969)
West Side Soul, Delmark

Jimmy Reed (1925–1976)
Blues Masters: The Very Best of Jimmy Reed, Rhino

Hubert Sumlin
I Know You, AcousTech

Muddy Waters (1915–1983)
His Best: 1947 to 1955 (Chess 50th Anniversary Collection), MCA/Chess

His Best: 1956 to 1964 (Chess 50th Anniversary Collection), MCA/Chess

w/Johnny Winter
Hard Again, Blue Sky

JAZZ BLUES

Charlie Christian (1916–1942)
The Genius of Electric Guitar Columbia

Grant Green (1931–1979)
The Best of Grant Green Blue Note

Kenny Burrell
Midnight Blue, Blue Note

BRIT BLUES & BLUES ROCK

Duane Allman (1946–1971)
Live at the Fillmore East Polydor

Michael Bloomfield (1943–1981)
w/The Paul Butterfield Blues Band
The Paul Butterfield Blues Band, Elektra

w/Al Kooper
Super Session, Sony

Eric Clapton
w/John Mayall
Blues Breakers with Eric Clapton, Deram

w/Cream
Fresh Cream, Universal

From the Cradle, Reprise

w/B.B. King
Riding with the King Warner Bros.

Peter Green
Green and Guitar: The Best of Peter Green 1977–1981 Music Club

Mick Taylor w/John Mayall
Crusade, London

TRAD REVIVAL & MODERN ELECTRIC

Rory Block
Gone Woman Blues, Rounder

Bob Brozman
A Truckload of Blues Rounder

Robert Cray
Heavy Picks: The Robert Cray Collection, Mercury

Robben Ford
Handful of Blues, Blue Thumb

David Hamburger
Indigo Rose, Chester

Corey Harris
Greens from the Garden Alligator

Alvin Youngblood Hart
Big Mama's Door Okeh/550 Music

Taj Mahal
The Best of Taj Mahal Sony Legacy

Keb' Mo'
Keb' Mo', Sony/550

Paul Rishell
I Want You to Know Tone-Cool

Joe Louis Walker
Bad Influence, Hightone

COLLECTIONS*

Blues Masters, Vol. 2: Post-War Chicago Blues

Blues Masters, Vol. 3: Texas Blues

Blues Masters, Vol. 8: Mississippi Delta Blues

Blues Masters, Vol. 15: Slide Guitar Classics

Blues Masters, Vol. 18: More Slide Guitar Classics

Chess Blues Guitar, MCA

The Greatest in Country Blues Volumes 1–3 Story of Blues

Guitar Player Presents: Legends of Guitar: Electric Blues, Vol. 1

Guitar Player Presents: Legends of Guitar: Electric Blues, Vol. 2

*All on Rhino

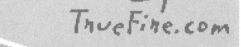